MARCH OF THE YEAR

MARCH OF THE YEAR

Especial Sermons for Special Days
by

G.   C U R T I S   J O N E S

THE   BETHANY   PRESS

ST. LOUIS

To

my immediate predecessors

F. W. BURNHAM

ROGER T. NOOE

HAMPTON ADAMS

to

my senior colleague

EDGAR DEWITT JONES

and to

my father-confessor

JOHN A. TATE

Foreword

G EORGE   B ERNARD   S HAW   gave up the position of drama critic on *The Saturday Review,* London, because of the frustration of recurring deadlines. He likened it
to fighting a windmill.

This is the prevailing dilemma of the preacher. Before he
regains his footing from one encounter, he is confronted with
another. He is forever flattened by the windmill of "special
days." Every minister conquers the calendar or is overwhelmed by it. World events, national observances, chamber
of commerce promotion, denominational directives, community and church schedules all increase the possibilities and
problems of preaching.

Amid the growing complexities of parish life, the minister
is continually faced with the demands of seasonal and special
observances. An examination of proposed emphases, as pro-
jected by religious councils and denominational agencies, reveals that approximately half the Sundays of a year are desig-
nated "special days."

High and holy days as observed by the average church are
a perennial challenge. Every minister, worker, and worshiper

7

needs help in preparing for stated occasions. This is a book of "special-day" sermons. Whereas preaching can never be reduced or completely transferred to the printed page, the homilies comprising this volume were preached from the pulpit of Union Avenue Christian Church, St. Louis, Missouri.

The first message in this volume is based on my article, "Beginning Again," which appeared in the January 2, 1957, issue of *The Christian-Evangelist*. Permission to use this material is appreciated.

The section entitled *Starting Blocks* is offered to assist minister and lay speakers in selecting appropriate subjects and Scriptures for presenting Christ throughout the calendar.

I am indebted to Mrs. W. C. Collins, popular writer of St. Louis, for a critical reading of the material; to Marvin G. Osborn, Jr., Washington University, and Professor Lionel A. Whiston, Jr., Eden Theological Seminary, for editorial counsel. Authors and publishers of cited materials are acknowledged in the footnotes. Gratitude is extended my secretary, Mrs. L. E. Payne, for typing the manuscript.

G. C. J.

Contents

9

On Beginning Again

"Behold, I make all things new."

—*Revelation 21:5*

A couple came to my study for a premarital conference. They were rather typical middle-aged Americans. During the course of our conversation it was apparent that each
had been married. I am not particularly allergic to divorced
persons, yet I nevertheless try to acquaint myself with past
circumstances in an effort to evaluate the case in light of
Christian teachings.

As we were exploring the implications of the proposed marriage, I said to the lady, "Tell me about your former husband." Smilingly she pointed to the man facing me. "There he
is," she said. Before I could query the gentleman, he winked,
pointed to her, and made this comment: "We were married
once before several years ago. One thing led to another and
finally we got a divorce. Now we know we were wrong and
we want to start over again."

Arrangements for their remarriage were made. It was a very
intimate and satisfying wedding. More genuine tears were in
evidence than expensive garlands; more love shown than cock-
tails served.

Or again, here was a charming lady and one of the most loyal members of our church. Her children sparkled with obvious brilliance. Their faces shone with contagious warmth. Their actions revealed their culture. One Sunday after worship, this queenly soul was found weeping in a corridor. She was brought to my study. Gently, I sought to discover her difficulty. Years before her husband met with a frightful accident. Faithfully she had assumed the dual role of father and mother to her sons and daughters. I also knew that she was as free of martyrdom as anyone of my acquaintance. She lived so quietly that one would never suspect that she had suffered so deeply. As we talked she said, "I am not good enough to be a member of the church. . . . My past . . . ."

"My dear," I replied, "none of us is worthy of the church. It is not a company of saints, but a congregation of sinners. For many of us just to know you and all you have done is an inspiration."

"No, I am not worthy," she rejoined. "I have not been as active nor as good as I might have been, and I would like to be rebaptized and start over. Can you baptize me again?"

"Yes, certainly, but it is hardly necessary. You have been baptized. God knows your heart. This church and community know your life. I think this confession and renewal of faith will be honored and remembered by God."

"I do too," she replied, "but I want the church to know that I am endeavoring to be a finer person."

"Very well. Would you like to come forward some Sunday in an act of rededication?"

"Yes, I would like to come forward next Sunday, reaffirm my faith, and be baptized again!"

It was a privilege to have been God's servant in that dramatic and dedicated moment.

My telephone rang. The voice was that of a man. He was calling to say that when next I was in his neighborhood, he would appreciate a visit. I replied that I would be glad to see him at my earliest opportunity. There was a pause, then he anxiously added, "I had hoped it would be convenient today."

There is only one thing for the minister to say in that situation and I said it. "I will be over this afternoon."

As I drove over to his house, I thought about our conversation: What is wrong? He is relatively new in the church. He is a man of means. Have I offended him? What can it be? My mind ran the gamut until I arrived at his impressive address. At the door I paused, as I frequently do, to ask God's guidance.

My friend greeted me warmly, saying, "Come in. I'm glad to see you. We are alone." In one way it put me at ease and in another, it sharpened my suspense. However, like the fine businessman that he was, he quickly came to the point: "Pastor, you no doubt wonder why I called you. I guess I wonder myself. The fact is, I haven't been well and my conscience hurts me."

"Yes?"

"Yes. You see I have been pretty successful in my business. All three of our children are college graduates, married and doing well. But I don't feel too good about certain things. Both of our boys were fighter pilots in World War II. I know it was selfish, but I prayed without ceasing that they would return. I prayed for others too, but I especially prayed for our boys. During those hectic months, I promised God that if they came back, I would be a better churchman. I haven't kept my word.

"I once quit a church because our preacher persisted in preaching about tithing. I thought he was after my money. Now I see things differently and I want to be a Christian. I want to be a trustworthy steward. I have called you here to make this confession and to ask you to pray with me."

It was a memorable moment.

We prepared to pray. I asked my host to pray first. He said, "It won't be a pretty prayer, but I'll try." He began with this never-to-be-forgotten sentence: "Dear Lord, I consecrate myself to thee. I consecrate my life anew. Make me a better husband and father . . . and churchman."

His prayer was so searching and moving that I could scarcely speak when it was my turn to pray.

How well I remember the day I quit high school. The baseball coach and I had words. I was a much better baseball player than he realized and I told him so. I was proud of my courage. However, it was difficult to explain to my parents what had transpired. They were, as usual, patient and understanding. Father saw to it that I took my place next morning with the Negro hands on the place. Working was an exhilarating joy. I was particularly co-operative and creative. One, two, three days passed and Father did not mention my returning to school. "Good," I thought, "he is going to let me have my way."

But the fourth morning at breakfast, my agrarian father calmly announced: "Son, get ready, *we* are going to school." It was anything but pleasant news and the interview was not anticipated. Dad, being the quiet giant he was, went straight to the principal's office and confronted him with the problem. Needless to say, I was ashamed of myself. Both the coach and I made concessions and confessions. It was a turning point in my life.

Years later I stood proudly with my Yale class in Woolsey Hall. I knew with grateful pride that my father was in the audience. After the colorful ceremony, as soon as there was an opportunity, I said to him, "And to think I once wanted to quit school."

These common experiences are authenticated by the testimony of time. Why are they? Because centuries ago in a remote corner of the world during one of the many difficult times in man's history, a miracle occurred in Bethlehem—a miracle that marked the beginning of a new and ever-increasing conception of life. Palestine was the land of promise. Calendars were revamped, lives transformed, and countless souls discovered the meaning of new beginnings. Not only did ancient wise men depart "to their own country by another way" (Matthew 2:12), but all subsequent aspirants to the new life who experience the supreme encounter, return home another way.

In the Fourth Gospel, a pathetic woman of Sychar met Jesus by Jacob's well. One can imagine this Samaritan drawer of water was neither young nor old. Now she was at that place in life where one can either live or reminisce, turn forward or turn back the pages of ambition. There were traces of a lost radiance in her face; an overexposed likeness of a once lovely person. Hearing and believing the Great Physician, she was relieved of her past. Refreshed and redeemed, she joyously ran back to her village saying, " 'Come, see a man who told me all that I ever did. Can this be the Christ?' " (John 4:29.)

Again we read how this Saving Person of Galilee stood in quiet condemnation as self-righteous scribes and punctilious Pharisees unleashed their criticisms on a sinful woman who had been dragged into his presence. She was accused of committing adultery. The wise men reminded Jesus of the laws of Moses and of their customs. While the puritans gave vent to their feelings, our Lord "wrote with his finger on the ground." At last his trumpet-tongued voice was heard above the confusion of the critics, "Let him who is without sin among you be the first to throw a stone at her." (John 8:7.)

He resumed his writing in the sand.

There was silence. Then the shuffling of sandals in retreat. Demagogues who paraded as teachers, men who posed as magnificent moral specimens, moved out of sight. At last Jesus lifted his eyes and said, " 'Woman, where are they? Has no one condemned you?' " (John 8:10.)

"She said, 'No one, Lord.' "

"And Jesus said, 'Neither do I condemn you; go, and do not sin again.' " (John 8:11.)

Forgiveness is always the land of beginning again.

Then one day, of all places, this scintillating and hopeful gospel of Christ reached the ears and heart of a little man—short in stature and in popularity—perched in a sycamore tree near Jericho. Zacchaeus, money-changer and mischanger, made a noble confession. Though by the roadside, it would have honored the altar of any sanctuary. Listen to this penitent soul, " 'Behold, Lord, the half of my goods I give to the poor; and if I have defrauded any one of anything, I restore it fourfold.'

"And Jesus said to him, 'Today salvation has come to this house. . .' " (Luke 19:8-9.)

In our more humble moods, we refer to Jesus as the Carpenter of Nazareth. He specialized in rebuilding human beings. He knew all the sin spots and blind spots of the ages, of every harrowed heart. To all who believed, he gave them power to conquer and to begin again.

Leo Tolstoy, author of *War and Peace*, lives eternally in his novels. Long before the provocative motion picture he was saluted as one of the world's great writers. Throughout the latter decades of the nineteenth century Tolstoy's native Russia idolized him. Yet we read he was a miserable man. He exploited every virtue and explored every vice. In his own *Confessions* he said, "My life, a life of indulgences and desires, was meaningless and evil."

He had tried everything. At last he was a captive of depression. He contemplated suicide. So extreme was his despair that he was afraid to permit a rope (intended for use in case of fire) to remain in his closet lest in the long sleepless night he might hang himself. It was during this period of desperation that Tolstoy began taking long walks in the country. On one of these he discovered how joyfully the peasants performed their menial tasks. In them he observed an enviable serenity and hope.

Gradually he faced himself. Some years later God came to Tolstoy as he was alone in the woods. There he shed the grave clothes of doubt and donned the royal garments of faith. Afterwards, the noted writer declared: "To know God and to live is one and the same thing. God is life. Live seeking God and then you will not live without God."

The New Year is traditionally a time of high resolves and vocal intentions. Today this is even more imperative. If there was ever a time when we need to scrub our slates, make reparations for our reprisals, and offer penitence for our sins, it is now. It is essential to begin with God. In him we begin; in him we end.

The curtain of time has rung down on another year. No amount of agonizing will rewrite the witness of your life or mine. But God has brought us to the land of beginning again and through his grace we may yet experience a more perfect day.

All pilgrims should heed and be heartened by Isaiah's assurance,

> "though your sins are like scarlet, they shall be as
>   white as snow;
> though they are red like crimson, they shall become
>   like wool."—Isaiah 1:18.

This is not to be interpreted as "do-it-yourself psychiatry." You cannot accomplish it alone. Neither is it a soothing statement to bring us to what the late Edwin McNeill Poteat described as "relaxed tolerance." Rather, it is the challenge of the "disciplined fellowship." It is a challenge to put up the sword of selfishness. To throw away the quiver of aggressive arrows and instead humbly don "the whole armor of God." In spiritual surrender and trust we find strength.

Christianity is, as Paul Tillich reminds us, the message of the New Creation.

The New Being is not something that simply takes the place of the Old Being. But it is a renewal of the Old which has been corrupted, distorted, split and almost destroyed. But not wholly destroyed. Salvation does not destroy creation; but it transforms the Old Creation into a New one.[1]

The Apostle Paul was well acquainted with the drama of beginning again. Harken to the wisdom of one who knew the life of rebuff and rebellion. After being reconciled to God and man he boldly declared, "If any one is in Christ, he is a new creation; the old has passed away, behold, the new has come. All this is from God, who through Christ reconciled us to himself and gave us the ministry of reconciliation." (2 Corinthians 5:17-18.)

Then, behold, we are found doing new things, for the old has indeed passed away and the new has come.

Let us begin again with God who makes all things new.

---

[1]From *The New Being,* by Paul Tillich. Copyright 1956 by Charles Scribner's Sons. Used by permission.

The Best Years of Our Lives

. . . Teach us to number our days
that we may get a heart of wisdom.

—*Psalm 90:12*

The Best Years of Our Lives was a prize-winning motion picture based on MacKinley Kantor's play *Glory for Me*. It told the story of our brave men and women who gallantly served America in World War II, dramatically presenting their difficulties, sacrifices, and adjustments to civilian life. The production was filled with interesting people. Captain Fred Derry came home to discover that his beautiful wife had been unfaithful. The Stephenson family occupied a prominent place in the story. The hero, of course, was Homer Parrish (on the stage Hommer Mermels), a fine specimen of manhood from Boone City who lost both hands in the burning of his ship. To observe his tedious and determined effort to re-establish himself in society was an emotional experience worthy of remembrance.

Both the play and the picture provoke haunting questions. When are the best years of our lives? When are the green years? Some would say childhood. Others would name the years of romance and flirtation. Many would settle for the seasons of exceptional business. Still others would answer, "College and the day I met my companion." But when are the best years of one's life?

Karl R. Stolz in *Making the Most of the Rest of Life* reminds us of the normal periods through which an individual passes. There are, of course, conception, birth, childhood, and the delicate and difficult period of adolescence. This philosophical psychologist designates the years twenty-three to thirty-five as a time of domestic, economic, and vocational adjustment. Thirty-five to forty-five is usually a time when one begins to taste success. From forty-five to fifty-five is a decade of dedicated production. Fifty-five to sixty-five is normally a time of conservation; and at sixty-five, one usually thinks of retirement.

Life is progression in which each physical stage has its own peculiar characteristics. Moreover, at each period the individual has definite contributions to offer. Youth is more than a time of life as measured by birthdays. It is also a state of mind. Whereas years and worries wrinkle the skin; dissipation, dejection, and sin wrinkle the soul. When Emerson reviewed life he exclaimed, "No one is old until his soul turns gray."

Johann Strauss, Jr., composed his first waltz when he was about six. Keats died before he was thirty, but not before his poems had enriched the English language. John Wesley preached with remarkable effectiveness when he was past eighty. Alexander Campbell was said to be at his peak as a preacher when he was twenty-seven. I repeat, age is relative.

When are the best years of our lives? Are they not the years when we look up to life, like a child, starry-eyed before his hero? Are they not the years in which we dream and plan? When we thankfully partake of the red wine of sunrise, we are refreshed in the knowledge that this is the day which the Lord has made. The mighty wings of the morning fan our hearts with hope and set our steps to music. With joyous abandon, we join Byron in exclaiming:

The morn is up again, the dewy morn,
With breath all incense and with cheek all bloom.

When we live in the mood of ecstasy and expectancy, we move on tiptoe. We are challenged by nature and circumstance to reflect something of God's glory and we are indestructibly happy. Conscious as we are of the mysteries of life, we are more aware of the manifestations of God's enduring care. Irritations and inconsistencies of our colleagues, companions, and even ourselves, are swept into the closet of memories and securely locked. Only forgiveness has the key.

To look up to life is exciting. The boy lies awake anticipating the fishing trip. The athlete is tense as he anticipates his event. Lovers nervously and meticulously live for that memorable wedding day. Parents await the arrival of their first-born with awe and thanksgiving. Johnnie's first day at school brings back memories. The day when one officially begins his life's work is one milestone. That searching hour when we accept Christ as the Lord of our lives and identify ourselves with his church is another.

As we review our fleeting years, we are aware of the peculiar privileges and distinct assets of each and every period of life. The art of looking up to life is not relegated to age or sex, station or schooling, but is one of the secrets of abundant living.

When are the best years of our lives? Are they not our working years? George Macdonald, noted Scottish poet-preacher, once said, "The door into life generally opens behind us . . . the sole wisdom of [one] haunted with . . . the scent of unseen roses, is work." So it is! "Genius," said Matthew Arnold, "is mainly an affair of energy."

Certainly work comes as near being the panacea for our dreams and desires as any experience of life. It is the common altar of mankind. Through our work, we live and commend our faith. Walt Whitman said: "There is no trade or employment, but the young man following it may become a hero."

Men of genius and of gentleness have been men who embraced their work with enthusiasm and hope. It was true in biblical days, it is true today. Simon Peter was a fisherman; Matthew, a tax collector; Paul, a tent-maker; and Jesus, a carpenter.

Thomas A. Edison declared, "I never did anything worth doing by accident, nor did any of my inventions come by accident." Joseph Conrad spoke bluntly, but correctly, when he insisted, "A man is a worker. If he is not that, he is nothing."

Man not only finds himself in his work, but he expresses himself through his work. Therefore, in a sense, work is salvation. It saves us from ourselves. It suggests ways of giving ourselves away. Idleness is dangerous. It breeds deterioration. Much of present-day crime and delinquency is traceable to unemployment and exploited leisure time. As parents we are constantly challenged to teach our children responsibility. When we save them from struggle, we deny them strength. It may be true that Johnnie is too young to join a labor union and have a paying job, but he could sell papers, cut the grass, or wash the car. Jane may not qualify for public employment, but certainly she could wash the dishes, make the beds, and baby-sit. Whether selling newspapers or publishing, following a plow or standing in a pulpit, riding the range or penetrating the sound barrier, man at his best is busy.

Work does not end with one's inability to do physical labor. Irrespective of age, as long as one has his mental faculties, he can make a significant contribution to life. Whenever one senses his place in the scheme of things, be he young or old, and lends a hand to life, he is in his green years.

When are the best years of our lives? Are they not our generous years? Generosity is more than a gesture of gratitude, it is a mark of maturity. The more deeply we live, the more aware we become of the needs of others, the more generous we are with our talents and resources. George Eliot's pensive comment gives us pause, "One must be poor to know the luxury of giving." Louis Ginsberg expressed a profound truth when he wrote, "The only things we ever keep are what we give away."

Is not this the meaning of the story of the rich young man? The aspirant intercepted Jesus to ask, " 'Good Teacher, what must I do to inherit eternal life?' " (Mark 10:17.) In our common vernacular, he had everything! He was obviously attractive, poised, intelligently inquisitive, possessed a winsome personality and was financially independent. Quickly our Lord appraised the man. He "loved" him. Thoughtfully Jesus listened as the stranger recapitulated his qualifications for living. The Master replied, " 'You lack one thing; go, sell what you have, and give to the poor, and you will have treasure in heaven; and come, follow me.' " (Mark 10:21.)

This man had not been able to give away the best that he had. He played it safe and lost his soul. God loves generous people. Whoever holds back on God locks himself out of life. Generosity is not synonymous with age. It is the outpouring of a dedicated life.

When are the best years of our lives? Are they not the helpful years? Are they not distinguished by one's ability to interpret need and to respond appropriately?

Late one night many years ago, a man and his wife stopped at a small hotel in Philadelphia. The woman was ill. Her husband sought a comfortable room for the evening. Standing before the man at the desk, the couple made no demands. The stranger simply inquired if they had any accommodations. "Every room in the hotel is filled," replied the manager, "but I will give you mine." The courteous hotel man did not know whom he was befriending. Next morning, the appreciative guest called the manager to say, "You're the kind of man who should be at the head of a really great hotel. I'd like to build one for you. If that interests you, please get in touch with me sometime."

The guest was none other than William Waldorf Astor and the manager of the Philadelphia hotel was the late George C. Boldt who, as head of the Waldorf Astoria, enjoyed the reputation of being one of the outstanding hotel men in America.

When are the best years of our lives? Are they not the years spent with God in thoughtful and enthusiastic witness?

The late Bishop William A. Quayle declared that the tragedy of Rip Van Winkle was not merely the fact that he deserted his family for drink, but that he slept through the American Revolution with a loaded gun by his side and never fired a shot. Is it not equally true that in these intoxicating and exciting days through which we are passing, marked by strife, anxiety, global disturbances, economic problems, and political pettifogging, we sleep through the current revolution without taking part in the contest?

To find God is the beginning of life and to keep in daily communion with him is the essence of life. Worship is the supreme challenge and comfort of the Christian. It transcends every barrier.

I once stood by the bedside of an elderly woman who was quietly drifting over the horizon. Her nurse told me she was inarticulate and incoherent. Gently, I took her hand. There was but the slightest response. Then I offered a prayer in clear simple language. Much to my surprise, and to the utter amazement of the nurse, when I said "Amen," this valiant soul whispered, "Amen." A few hours later she was gone. Doubtless this dear one knew what Robert Browning meant when he said:

> Grow old along with me!
> The best is yet to be,
> The last of life for which the first was made!

The Battle for Brotherhood

Have we not all one father? Has not one God created us? Why then are we faithless to one another, profaning the covenant of our fathers?

—*Malachi 2:10*

M A N ' S   S T R U G G L E for supremacy and superiority started early. We see its cunning and cost in the conflict between Cain and Abel. They were the first sons of Adam and Eve. Both were born, however, after the garden episode. Strangely enough their enmity began about the altar of their stewardship. Cain earned his living by farming while Abel tended flocks. According to custom and faith, in due time, each brother brought an offering to the Lord. Cain presented the best from his fields while Abel gave God the first-born of his flock. The Lord preferred the sacrifice of Abel.

Immediately Cain rebelled. Feuding began and continued until Cain satisfied his contempt. At last he induced his brother to go with him into the fields and there he slew him. Then God said to the murderer, "Were is Abel your brother?"

"I do not know; am I my brother's keeper?"

"And the Lord said, 'What have you done? The voice of your brother's blood is crying to me from the ground.'" (Genesis 4:9-10.)

26

Cain could deny his kinship, but not the murder. Blood was dripping from his hands.

Kinsmen and distant relatives continue to resent one another and to retaliate. Family disaffection reminds us of the tragedy of sin and of the infinite patience of God. If blood relatives find it difficult to maintain Christian admiration and respect, how much more difficult it becomes for God's scattered family to live in harmony and good will. Brotherhood begins at home or it never begins.

Among the papers and writings of the late F. Scott Fitzgerald was found the plot for an unwritten play. It centered about five widely separated members of a family who would inherit a stately house if they agreed to live in it together. This, of course, is more than a figment of Fitzgerald's imagination. Though this play was never written, it must be written if we are to survive. Either we must quickly learn the lessons of brotherhood or we shall soon hear the committal services for those we love.

What the LORD said to Cain is both pertinent and disturbing: "'Why are you angry, and why has your countenance fallen? If you do well, will you not be accepted? And if you do not do well, sin is couching at the door; its desire is for you, but you must master it.'" (Genesis 4:6-7.)

History is not only stippled with struggles between kinsmen and individuals in their determination to gain recognition or to retaliate; society itself is stamped with its defiance of brotherhood. Toward the end of Harry S. Ashmore's definitive and brilliant book, *An Epitaph for Dixie*, he refers to the South's history "as something of a personal tragedy. But it seems to me that the tragedy lies not in the battles we lost, but in the battles we never fought."[1]

[1]From *An Epitaph for Dixie*, by Harry S. Ashmore. Copyright 1957, 1958 by W. W. Norton & Company, Inc. Used by permission.

This is in reality the tragedy of history. Every honest citizen and Christian from every race and clan, neighborhood and country, would be compelled to say that the tragedy of the human race is not the battles lost, but the battles men refuse to fight. The world would have us believe that the great battle is to conquer outer space or a national enemy. On the contrary, the great battle is to convert the hearts of men to the will of Christ lest conflagration consume the human race.

In commenting on Governor Orval Faubus' stand on the integration of Central High School in Little Rock, Mr. Ashmore wrote: "Perhaps the most charitable thing that could be said of the Arkansas governor was that he misunderstood the past, miscalculated the present and ignored the future."[2] Is this not a common failure? What advantage would it be if we should gain dominance in intercontinental missiles and leave men to grope for hope on the streets of your community and mine? " 'For what will it profit a man, if he gains the whole world and forfeits his life?' " (Matthew 16:26.)

The battle for brotherhood in America has been and continues to be a thrilling and disturbing chapter in our courageous history. The fifteenth century is generally accepted as an era of intellectual revolution. The sixteenth century is permanently remembered as the century of religious revolution. The seventeenth century was one of social revolution, and the eighteenth century is recorded as one of tremendous political revolution which included the revolt of the colonies and the framing of the American Constitution. The nineteenth century was the era of our industrial revolution. Whatever else time may dictate, the twentieth century will be remembered as the century of human revolution. Will civilization be cremated or will it be re-created in the knowledge and love of Almighty God? Will the twentieth century be the century of despair?

---

[2]*Ibid.*

The battle of brotherhood in America originates out of the exploitation of the Indians and the establishment of slavery. The human struggle speaks of the splendor and sorrow of ante-bellum days. The Dred Scott decision of 1857 is clearly written in our history as well as May 17, 1954, the date of the Supreme Court's decree relative to the desegregation of public schools. Reverberations from Montgomery, Little Rock, Chicago, Norfolk and the school scandals in New York City speak for themselves. It should also be remembered that one-fourth of the public schools in seventeen Southern and border states desegregated without serious incident. Add to the roll call of twentieth-century human relations that in Delaware the Finance Minister of Ghana was refused dining privileges.

Observe the rise of White Citizens' Councils; tightly knit neighborhoods; the emergence of mutual admiration societies; the return of the Ku Klux Klan; and the righteous conservatism of a vast number of churchmen. All have come in for comment and criticism. The battle against brotherhood is fiercely fought.

America's march on brotherhood must also be told in terms of the tremendous progress made in cultural relations: more jobs for minority people; more social acceptance; more freedom than ever before; and unaccustomed votes from once forgotten people now turn the tide in public elections. The past twenty years has produced a social fermentation unlike that of any other period in recorded history. Dr. Ralph Bunche, Undersecretary of the Department of Trusteeship of the United Nations, reminds us that in 1939, some 750,000,000 people, approximately one-third of mankind, all nonwhite, were under colonial rule of one kind or another. Today only 150,000,000, mostly in Africa, and they are revolting, are so restricted. A social structure which required some 300 years to establish, is rapidly disintegrating. Even with the Soviet's subtle invasion of many sectors of the world, these are amazing accomplishments.

It is strange that professing Christians who confess to the Fatherhood of God and who claim to believe in the brotherhood of man, find it so difficult to practice. The problem of human relations is a universal problem and unless we can solve it, all other problems are futile. In the South it is the battle between the white and the Negro; in the Southwest it is the Anglo-Saxon and the Mexican; in the Far West it is the problem of the Oriental; while in the Northwest it centers around the Indian. Wherever there are sizeable minority groups there will be anti-Semitism, anti-Catholicism, or anti-Protestantism. I found discrimination in Australia, Egypt, Malaya, Thailand, India, and Palestine. We are not talking about a sectional problem; we are voicing a universal concern which has in it the salvation of peace or the seeds of war.

Consider the incredible story of the good Samaritan. The young man's pensive question concerning neighborliness prompted Jesus to speak on human solidarity. In commenting on the provocative parable, Stephen F. Bayne says, "Samaritan or Jew, believer or nonbeliever, good or bad, black or white, there is no way for us to shake off the reality of brotherhood. We may curse it. We may try to run away from it. But there is no way to deny it."[3]

"If any one says, 'I love God,' and hates his brother, he is a liar; for he who does not love his brother whom he has seen, cannot love God whom he has not seen." (1 John 4:20).

Springfellow Barr challenges America to join the human race. He reminds us of the prenatal climate of chance. A baby

---

[3]From *In the Sight of the Lord,* by Stephen F. Bayne. Copyright 1958 by Harper & Brothers. Used by permission.

born any year has less than one chance in twenty of being born in the United States and not more than one in three of being born white.

People are our problem. They are also our hope.

We would do well to rethink the ancient story of Joseph who was sold by his brothers. They lied to their father and old Jacob grieved for his favorite son. Under Pharaoh, Joseph rose to prominence. At last the famine-licked brothers stood before the courageous ruler of Egypt. Joseph recognized them, but they did not know him. One of the dramatic moments in the story was when the governor insisted that their younger brother, Benjamin, should appear. His stinging comment was, " 'You shall not see my face, unless your brother is with you.' " (Genesis 43:3.)

Nor shall we see God's!

James Truslow Adams in *The Epoch of America* insists that a unique distinction of our country has been its frontiers. Noble men have accepted them. However, as the late Rufus M. Jones maintained, our land frontiers are gone: "We must discover a new skyline, new frontiers of life, and creative faith." In this climate and in this mood the follower of Christ is challenged to find and to behold his brother.

Another disturbing and obvious area of distorted brotherhood is in the church itself. Denominationalism is indeed a glaring sin. It is of man's choosing, not God's design. There is one Lord, one faith, and one church. If brotherhood is to be restored, the community of forgiveness established, and love become the law of life, then the church must epitomize the ideal.

The church must lead. The winds of God are mighty and they are blowing through the churches with refreshing reminders of our common faith. The witness to man's essential oneness and faith by such groups as the National and World Council of Churches and their constituent bodies is encouraging. The unity of God's people may be nearer at hand than we realize. Let those who have borne the brunt of the battle take heart. As in all conflicts there are martyrs and heroes, the homeless and homed, but let no one desert the battle. Let no one become victim of his own ambitions, nor fear the outcome of the struggle. Rather let us all put our trust in him who lived above the connivings and complacency of men. Let the church become the pattern of brotherhood, not the perverter.

The Minister's Black Veil is a disturbing story. In it Nathaniel Hawthorne tells of a day when the sexton in a Milford meetinghouse stood tolling the bell for worship. At last the humble man of God appeared. "But what has good Parson Hooper got upon his face?" With this the crowd turned and beheld their leader meditatively walking toward the house of prayer with a black veil around his face. His forehead, eyes, and nose were covered.

"Are you sure it is our pastor?" asked Goodman Gray.

"Of a certainty it is good Mr. Hooper," replied the sexton.

The congregation was aghast, irritated, and perplexed as the pastor mounted the stairs of the high pulpit. What was he concealing? The clergyman's covered face quickly became the topic of conversation throughout the community. Even children voiced their ideas as they walked to school.

Against all counsel, even that of his gentle wife, Mr. Hooper lived out his life, performing the duties of his office with a veiled face.

Years passed and at last Mr. Hooper lay on his deathbed. The swathe of black crepe still concealed his face. Friends and relatives came to comfort him in his final illness. Among them was young Mr. Clark, a zealous minister from Westbury. All attempts to remove the veil were in vain. Suddenly as if he rallied to register his last complaint, Mr. Hooper broke the silence by exclaiming, "I look around me, and, lo! On every visage a black veil!"

Hawthorne concludes with this comment, "The grass of many years has sprung up and withered on that grave, the burial-stone is moss-grown, and good Mr. Hooper's face is dust; but awful is still the thought that it mouldered beneath the black veil!"

As brothers and fellow Christians, let us remove our veils and look with charity, clarity, and confidence to the One who lived the covenant of our fathers.

"Have we not all one father? Has not one God created us? Why then are we faithless to one another, profaning the covenant of our fathers?"

Is It Nothing to You?

"Is it nothing to you, all you who pass by?"
                              —Lamentations 1:12

T H E R O P E dangled in the breeze. It hung from the limb of a giant oak tree. A curious crowd enveloped the country store. The people had come, not to barter nor to buy but to witness a heinous crime. A Negro, accused of murdering a storekeeper, had been apprehended and hanged. His lifeless body lay in the store of that small Virginia community. Remembrances of that scene remain as grotesque as when first I viewed it as a boy.

As we drove homeward, my father said, "Son, today you have seen what madmen will do. The first murder was bad enough without adding another. I hope you will never be party to any such thing." His manner and words greatly impressed me. In my heart I wished we had arrived earlier. Perhaps my strong father and others like him could have thwarted the tragedy.

However horrible this memory, it is not to be compared with what happened on a hill outside Jerusalem. There, not a criminal, but the Christ; not a lawless murderer, but the Lamb of God was slain.

What, then, is the meaning of this cruel cross standing against the horizon of history? What possible connection could there be between the erection of that Roman cross in the year thirty-five and the salvation of men today? Prophetically pertinent are the words out of Lamentations in which the poet wept over Jerusalem: "Is it nothing to you, all you who pass by?"

The cross was inevitable. This is not to suggest theological sleight of hand nor that the crucifixion was a predestined act from which Jesus could not extricate himself. Not at all, for he was free. His love and faithfulness to the Father and to men, constrained him to face the cross.

Jesus was certain to encounter opposition. He was too daring, too devoted, to go unnoticed. In our less logical moments, we vehemently accuse the Jews of crucifying our Lord. In a similar mood, they have frequently placed the blame on the Romans. No one can hope to understand the cross, however vaguely, with such an unintelligent approach. It would be just as logical to blame the Romans for killing Cicero, or the Greeks for giving Socrates the cup of hemlock, or the people of India for shooting Gandhi, or Americans for assassinating Lincoln! The cross points to no particular people but rather to the sinful nature of all peoples.

It was inevitable that the conservative and privileged Sadduccees, who were more interested in a secular society than a spiritual kingdom, should rise up against this adventuresome man of Galilee. These aristocrats had much to do with the crucifixion. The privileged in economics, culture, and learning have always been slow to accept the will and the way of God.

Once I stood in Carey's Chapel, Calcutta, listening to the pastor retell the courageous life of that noble pioneer. As never before his life took on new light for me. But have Christians forgotten that in 1789, when William Carey announced that he was going as a missionary to India, the East India Company vigorously protested? It was considered imprudent. An idealistic missionary might jeopardize the high profits of their investments. Every generation has its Sadduccees, guardians of the *status quo,* coiners of the temple tax, who persist in protecting their invested interests.

The crucifixion was inevitable because of the Pharisees. They were the most representative religious group of Palestinian Judaism. Their influence far exceeded their numerical strength. They were good people. They believed in God, in prayer, in the resurrection. Whereas Jesus was not identified with any ecclesiastical body, he was very close to the Pharisees. But as is frequently the case, these good people became his bitter enemies. They gossiped, they accused, they incited cunning treachery. These legalistically minded churchmen could not bear to see the new Teacher transcend their laws and traditions.

Jesus was not deceived by their conduct nor was he afraid of the consequences. Some of his sharpest utterances were directed to the Pharisees. " 'Woe to you, scribes and Pharisees, hypocrites! because you shut the kingdom of heaven against men; for you neither enter yourselves, nor allow those who would enter to go in.' " (Matthew 23:13.)

" 'You serpents, you brood of vipers, how are you to escape being sentenced to hell?' " (Matthew 23:33.)

Yes, leaders of state and temple, celebrities and custodians of the faith, put Jesus to death. The clash was inevitable. The Son of endless light was certain to disturb the sons of darkness. In *Behold the Glory,* Chad Walsh says, "Darkness *must* shape itself into a cross. A cross is the meaning of darkness."

The cross was voluntarily accepted. Jesus was not conscripted as was Simon of Cyrene. Out of love he carried his cross. Our Master was impelled to bear the glorious message

of God at whatever cost. This explains that, though crucifix-
ions were common in the first century, we remember only the
crosses that were planted at Golgotha.

To the weeping women who edged the path to Calvary,
Jesus said, " 'Daughters of Jerusalem, do not weep for me, but
weep for yourselves and for your children.' " (Luke 23:28.)
In the words of the Fourth Gospel he declared, " 'For this reason the Father loves me, because I lay down my life, that I
may take it again. No one takes it from me, but I lay it down
of my own accord. I have power to lay it down, and I have
power to take it again; . . .' " (John 10:17-18.)

Here we see the freedom and generosity of love. Voluntary
acts are always more meaningful than assigned duties. This
voluntary cross, the centerpiece of the centuries, is the standard of Christian living. It is as real as rain and as sharp as
lightning. No one can serve two masters. The Christian must
take his stand and bear witness to his faith. Love is the bond
that binds us together and leads us to God. And the love that
came down from the cross compels a response. We cannot
escape the decision to accept or reject the cross.

Sometimes we refer to our burdens and superimposed responsibilities as crosses. Caring for an invalid, living with a
handicap, are frequently considered crosses. Whereas these
experiences reveal strength of character, they are not crosses.
Any gentleman will do what he has to do, but the Christian
will do gladly what he does not have to do. We gain courage
for our tasks from the vision of Calvary. Jesus charged his
followers to accept a cross and follow.

Whenever the voluntary nature of the cross is mentioned, I
am reminded of a noted university professor whose brilliant
brother, a practicing physician, died suddenly. The philosopher's love for his brother was so genuine that he took leave

for several months to become better acquainted with medicine in order to be a congenial and intelligent companion with his brother's friends.

I remember a young businessman, well along in his thirties, who felt the call of the Christian ministry. He resigned from his business, sold his home, and entered college to prepare for his heart's desire. He and his family joyfully accepted their cross.

Briant, the famous Flemish sculptor, was extremely poor. He frequently went without food and worked in a clammy studio. It was bitter cold the night he finished his statuette of Mercury. The thoughtful and meticulous artist was concerned lest the firm, fresh clay of his creation should freeze and crack. He had too much of himself in the design to run the risk of its being ruined, so he wrapped it in his warmest coat.

Briants died from exposure during the night. His cherished statuette was found unharmed. The warmth of sacrifice had saved it. In some such thoughtful way, beyond our ability to imagine or conceive, the cross is God's voluntary cloak of sacrifice spread in mercy over his creation.

> See, from His head, His hands, His feet,
> Sorrow and love flow mingled down;
> Did e'er such love and sorrow meet,
> Or thorns compose so rich a crown?
>
> Were the whole realm of nature mine,
> That were a present far too small;
> Love so amazing, so divine,
> Demands my soul, my life, my all.
>
> —Isaac Watts

The cross has made it impossible for us to forget Jesus Christ. From it we see suffering and redeeming love. Far more significant than the cross as a symbol, or as a design, is the fact that the spirit of the cross is immersed in the universe. As Emerson put it, "Jesus is not so much written in human history as ploughed into it." The cross is God's ploughshare.

We can never forget that through the miracle of the cross God uniquely and persuasively entered the human heart. Here we see the misery of man transcended by the glory of God. "For Jews demand signs and Greeks seek wisdom, but we preach Christ crucified, a stumbling-block to Jews and folly to Gentiles, but to those who are called, both Jews and Greeks, Christ the power of God and the wisdom of God." (1 Corinthians 1:22-25.)

There was something so miraculous yet meaningful about the constraining cross that Paul wrote to the Galatians, "But far be it from me to glory except in the cross of our Lord Jesus Christ, . . ." (Galatians 6:14.) Imagine anyone saying today, "Far be it from me that I should glory except in the gas chamber, or the gallows, or the hangman's knot, or the electric chair!" That which elevated Golgotha's act fom the gruesome to the glorious was the presence and power of God. He had the last word and his will shook the world.

We can never forget that on the cross Jesus demonstrated that there can be no lasting love without genuine suffering. The physician and the nurse suffer with their patients. The parent suffers with his child.

The sufferings of our day are tied up with self-pity; we need the cleansing power of therapeutic suffering.

Norman Vincent Peale maintains that Americans require more than 7,000,000 sleeping pills every night. From Washington, D. C., comes the report that approximately 12,000,000 pounds of aspirin are sold annually.

We suffer from many things; plans gone awry, dreams shattered, business disappointments, family anxieties, health and money problems, and many, many other concerns. The strong, helpful individual is usually the one who is acquainted with our sufferings, with our problems, with our apprehensions.

Yes, the cross keeps Christ constantly before us. It reminds us that life cannot rise to its heights without sacrifice and suffering. The way of the cross is the way to God.

The cross connotes forgiveness. Man could not live without forgiveness. He is too weak to face his responsibilities without the replenishment and refreshment that comes from forgiveness. As is true with nearly every institution, Judaism in the time of Jesus had come to look at life with legalistic eyes. Simon Peter, looking through the prisms of legalism, once inquired of Jesus, " 'Lord, how often shall my brother sin against me, and I forgive him? As many as seven times?' " (Matthew 18:21.) To this the Master replied, " 'I do not say to you seven times, but seventy times seven.' " (Matthew 18:22.) There was no limit save that of love. In fact our Lord declared that unless we forgive those who trespass against us we cannot hope for our heavenly Father to forgive us our trespasses.

The cross bears witness to eternal forgiveness. Reconciliation is impossible without forgiveness. One cannot be reconciled to God without first being reconciled to his fellow man. Forgiveness is the key that unlocks the door to new life. How remote to the unbeliever then and now are the words from the cross, " 'Father, forgive them; for they know not what they do.' " (Luke 23:34.)

As a young minister, I frequently preached at road camps, commonly referred to as "chain gangs." Once, while speaking on the necessity of forgiveness, I noticed that tears filled the eyes of a burly man. Later, the guard told me this man desired a conference. When it was granted, the conversation ran something like this:

"I thought you said that whatever the sin, God would forgive. Is that right?"

"Yes," I replied, "if you satisfactorily meet the requirements of forgiveness and then demonstrate the new life in Christ."

"Well, I killed a man. I can't get him off my mind. . . ."

He began to weep. He told me the whole story. I suggested certain passages of Scripture, daily disciplines, and acts of penance. We prayed together during which time he reiterated his guilt to God.

Some weeks later after service, the guard told me the man wanted to know if I would eat dinner with him. This prisoner was one of the chefs. He prepared a good meal and I complimented him on his culinary skills. To which he replied, "Thank you for telling me the story of forgiveness."

If the cross brings hope and peace to a convicted murderer, what can it not mean to every man?

The cross assures us that we have a Savior. It vividly reminds us that the sinful plans of men could not overthrow the divine plans of God. "They put him to death by hanging him on a tree; but God raised him on the third day and made him manifest; . . ." (Acts 10:39-40.)

We need a Savior—we who are tempted and burdened and perplexed. We need to feed our minds and hearts on the life of the One who was tempted even as are we, but who lived and died victoriously and who lives forever in the hearts of believers.

An English writer once said that every man struggling to succeed in the literary world should write with an eye on the far-off island where Robert Louis Stevenson lived. So through the continuing centuries, all who have sought salvation have kept their minds and hearts focused on Calvary. There is more here than we can comprehend, but we can understand enough to know that we have been bought with a price.

I confess that at times the atonement posed great problems for me. This is especially true of those theories that deal with the bizarre blood-bank conception of salvation, in which the cross is a bloody sacrifice to appease an angry God. However, at last it broke upon me that it was not altogether necessary that I be able to present systems of thought fully explaining the subject. It was not for me to explain, but to proclaim God's saving grace.

Those of us who have been privileged to "walk in his steps," can testify to the emotion that captures one when he stands where tradition says Jesus was crucified. It is soul searching. In such a moment he recalls, with some sense of guilt, the truth of Harold Phillips' words: "One great weakness of the Christian church is that in the realm of belief we strut, while in the realm of action we straddle."[1]

Calvary is the place of action. God shattered the spear and the sword. The temple was rent. Love was enthroned.

---

[1]From *In the Light of the Cross*. Copyright 1947 by Abingdon Press.

What Death Cannot Do

"I am the resurrection and the life; he who believes in me, though he die, yet shall he live, and whoever lives and believes in me shall never die. Do you believe this?"

—*John 11:25-26*

H E L O O K E D as old as the Judean hills and just as ugly. A short stocky man draped in soiled robes stood at the entrance to Lazarus' tomb. Beneath his weathered face was a contagious smile. His clear piercing eyes flashed the confirmation of Easter. Proudly he spoke of Bethany. With deep feeling, he described the sadness that claimed the community when Lazarus died. Gently he pointed to the tombs, saying, "Jesus came here and raised Lazarus. This is the place where the Master said, 'I am the resurrection and the life.'" So spoke the guide on my visit to Bethany.

Bethany was never the same, nor was the world. With the raising of Lazarus came also the indestructible faith in the redeeming power of Jesus Christ. Easter reminds us that just over the hills from the home of Mary and Martha our Lord's own resurrection gave final confirmation to the miracle.

The resurrection of Jesus reassures us that death has been conquered. What a contrast between the cowed disciples on dark Friday and the awed apostles on Easter morning. From Calvary they fled in fear.

Man has always feared death. He has more faith in physical protection than spiritual security. To walk amid the pyramids of Egypt is to realize they are ancient tombs, elaborately equipped for special residence in the next world. Only a great fear of the unknown would cause a king to labor a lifetime to assure himself of survival. Death has been memorialized through the centuries.

Philip II, king of Macedon and father of Alexander the Great, gave one of his servants a strange though significant assignment. Every morning the slave would parade into the presence of the king and solemnly announce, "Remember, Philip, thou must die."

We all need to remember this declaration. However camouflaged, however inoffensive, death is an irrefutable reality. Much is made over it; sometimes funeral displays far excel demonstrations of Christian discipleship. Extravagant sentimentality frequently prevails. The mortuary is a house of death, not a house of life. When a family decides to have the service of memory for a loved one either in their home or in their church, they bear witness to their Christian faith. The home and the church are dedicated to life, not death.

The miracle of the resurrection should dispel morbid concepts of death and discourage pagan observances of funerals. The occasion of one's home-going should be lifted to a high and holy plane of worship. What we erroneously call death is in reality rebirth. Death is man's final ascension. He is freed of time and space dimensions. He is relieved of physical encumbrances and promoted to active eternal life.

When Jesus and his disciples came to the city of Nain, they met a funeral procession. There was genuine sorrow. A widow had lost her only son. When the Lord saw the distraught woman, he was filled with compassion and charged her not to weep. "And he came and touched the bier, and the bearers stood still. And he said, 'Young man, I say to you, arise.' And the dead man sat up, and began to speak. And he gave him to his mother." (Luke 7:14-15.)

Jesus met death in the gate of the city. This is the way God planned it. Death and life always meet in a narrow place. Thus death never escapes the transforming touch of Christ.

Nancy Byrd Turner invites us to see death as the gateway to a fuller life:

> Death is only an old door
>   Set in a garden wall.
> On gentle hinges it gives at dusk,
>   When the thrushes call.
>
> Along the lintel are green leaves,
>   Beyond, the light lies still;
> Very weary and willing feet
>   Go over that sill.
>
> There is nothing to trouble any heart,
>   Nothing to hurt at all.
> Death is only an old door
>   In a garden wall.[1]

In the words of our living Lord, "I am the resurrection and the life; he who believes in me, though he die, yet shall he live, and whoever lives and believes in me shall never die."

The resurrection of Jesus should reassure us that truth is indestructible. Like the seeds of spring it is forever coming to life. Doubtless the Pharisees, as they walked by Joseph's tomb in Arimathea, felt the Master dead and done with. They must have been inarticulate on Easter morning when Jerusalem literally vibrated with the echo, "He has risen!"

---

[1] "Death Is a Door." Reprinted by permission of Dodd, Mead & Co. from *Star in a Well*, by Nancy Byrd Turner. Copyright 1935 by Dodd, Mead & Co. Also by permission of Good Housekeeping Magazine.

Proud and powerful Romans tried to bury Christianity in prisons and catacombs, but it rose up and conquered the unconquerable.

While in prison John Bunyan produced *Pilgrim's Progress* with the unforgettable Christian and his companion, Faithful.

Mahatma Gandhi knew imprisonment and suffering, but his spirit soared above his surroundings. He meant it as a great compliment to our Lord when he declared that the man who had impressed him most had never set foot on India's soil.

Martin Niemöller was one of Hitler's prized prisoners. The famous German minister vigorously resisted tyranny. He was imprisoned for seven and a half years. He was interned at a camp where, during the seven years, 238,756 persons were put to death. Yet he carried on a daring ministry at Dachau.

Pastor Niemöller is more than a former prisoner of war. He is a living testimony to truth. To talk with Niemöller is to visit a man who looked death in the face day after day and knew the power of the resurrected Christ. His remarkable life reassures us of the triumph of truth.

James Russell Lowell speaks with pertinency:

> Though the cause of evil prosper,
> Yet 'tis truth alone is strong:
> Though her portion be the scaffold,
> And upon the throne be wrong;
> Yet that scaffold sways the future,
> And, behind the dim unknown,
> Standeth God within the shadow
> Keeping watch above His own.

Truth is the substance of life. The Greeks were among the earliest explorers of truth. Pilate's question is the question of each successive generation, " 'What is Truth?' " (John 18:38.) If asked, everyone would claim to be on a pilgrimage for truth. At first the child accepts authoritarian truth. Later he rebels. Carefully adults try to avoid truth. Paul Tillich maintains there are two normal ways to evade truth: "The one is the way of those who claim to have the truth and the other is the way of those who do not care for truth."[2]

Truth is more than the accumulation of fact. It is ultimate wisdom. Truth is more than a doctrine or belief; it is a way of life. Jesus himself said, "I am the way, and the truth, . . ." (John 14:6.) We usually think of truth in terms of statements and declarations. But the Gospel equates truth with life. "I am the way, and the truth, and the life; no one comes to the Father, but by me." (John 14:6.)

On this Easter morning, above every other truth we want to accept the Lord's exclamation: "I am the resurrection and the life; he who believes in me, though he die, yet shall he live, and whoever lives and believes in me shall never die."

The resurrection of Jesus should increase and strengthen our faith in God. The One who created is capable of preserving. As Dr. Fosdick said in *On Being Fit to Live With,* "This, then, is at stake on Easter Day: Is this a universe that keeps its lowest and lets its highest go?" It is unthinkable that a merciful Father would preserve the mountains and the hills, the fields and the forest, through the centuries, and permit the noblest of his creation—man—to evaporate into nothingness with the expiration of visible life. This would make God a reckless Father. Therefore, the real question before us is not: Can we trust God with our lives beyond the grave? The embarrassing query is: Can God trust us with life before the grave? Indeed, faith is the victory!

Roy Burkhart says, "Faith is the brave hypothesis of which life is the brave experiment."

---

[2]Tillich, *op. cit.*

Paul referred to faith as the substance of hope. Faith is always living as if something were true, in order to prove it.

The scientist believes that the physical universe is trustworthy. A farmer has faith that the seed will germinate and that God's laws of growth and seasonal rhythm will continue. The businessman has faith in his product and his ability to sell it. A research doctor has faith to believe that the dreaded disease will yet be conquered. Travelers have faith that those who operate airlines will also employ reliable personnel. Therefore, they board planes without interviewing the pilot. Lovers have faith in each other, and homes are started.

Just so, the Christian will conjure in his heart the pattern of life found in Jesus and commit himself to it. Though he may never attain it, he will believe in it and constantly match his life against its message.

In London during World War II a placard, hung over broadcasting booths, read, "Is what you are saying worth a man's risking his life to hear?" Jesus not only risked his life, indeed, he gave it for the privilege of saying, "I am the resurrection and the life; he who believes in me, though he die, yet shall he live, and whoever lives and believes in me shall never die."

The resurrection of Jesus should reassure us that our Lord is eternally alive. Once when plaguing problems and difficult decisions beset Martin Luther, he was seen to write on the dust of a table top, "He is alive, he lives!" This is the quintessence of Easter. Christ is triumphantly alive in our world; and because he lives, we, too, shall live.

Let us not, therefore, busy ourselves with mystic details of the future, but rather in living the good life. Reinhold Niebuhr once said, "It is unwise for Christians to claim any knowledge of either the furniture of heaven or the temperature of hell." For as Paul put it,

. . . "no eye has seen, nor ear heard,
nor the heart of man conceived,
what God has prepared for those who love him."

—1 Corinthians 2:9

Jesus is alive in every heart and in every home where love lives.

Love is the carrier of life.

Elizabeth Fry lives in every conscientious effort to improve prison conditions. The Wright brothers live in every plane that pierces the blue. James Watt lives in every steam plant. Thomas Jefferson comes to life in every brilliantly drawn judicial document. Abraham Lincoln is compassionately alive in every constructive effort to liberate the oppressed. Gutenberg lives in every best-seller. Homer speaks in every polished poem, and David sings in every great hymn. Louis Pasteur is praised in every glass of milk. Guglielmo Marconi is heard in every broadcast. The spirit of William Carey lives in every missionary. The anonymous Samaritan of the Scriptures is revealed in ministries of mercy. Mary, the mother of Jesus, lives in dedicated mothers and trustful Joseph is remembered in good fathers. Jesus lives wherever there is faith to believe he is alive.

The resurrection of Jesus reassures us of the glorious morning of the endless day. There is always something wonderfully promising about the morning. It is filled with hope.

> Listen to the Exhortation of the Dawn!
> Look to this Day!
> For it is Life, the very Life of Life.
> In its brief course lie all the
> Verities and Realities of your Existence:
>
> The Bliss of Growth,
> The Glory of Action,
> The Splendor of Beauty,

For Yesterday is but a Dream,
And To-morrow is only a Vision:
But To-day well-lived makes
Every Yesterday a Dream of Happiness,
And every To-morrow a Vision of Hope.
Look well therefore to this Day!
Such is the Salutation of the Dawn![3]

There was never a morning like the one that flooded the world with the light of eternal day. The Marys in their love visited the sepulchre. Their eyes were too full of tears to see the purple sunrise, their hearts too heavy to envision returning and rejoicing disciples. Unseeing they passed through the garden of Arimathea until at last they neared the tomb. Then came this voice,

" 'You need not be afraid. I know that you are looking for Jesus who was crucified. He is not here, he has risen, as he said he would do. Come and see the place where he was lying. Now go quickly and tell his disciples. . . .' " (Matthew 28: 5-6.)[4]

The women left the tomb, frightened yet overjoyed. And as they ran to spread the news, Jesus himself met them and said, " 'Good morning!' " (Matthew 28:9.) Indeed, it was the greatest morning in the history of man. It is knowledge of and belief in that morning that enables us to face the night of death.

Christ is not a dead hero we salute, but a Living Lord we serve. Those who experienced the thrill and stimulation of that Easter morning in Jerusalem had no difficulty believing he was alive. So to countless millions through the ages he has been, and is today, a living Lord, Savior, and Companion, whom to know is life eternal.

---

[3]"The Salutation of the Dawn," a poem based on the Sanskrit, c. 1200 B.C.

[4]From *The Bible: An American Translation,* by J. M. Powis Smith and Edgar Goodspeed. Used by permission of the University of Chicago Press.

The Pentagon and Pentecost

When the day of Pentecost had come, they were all together in one place. And suddenly a sound came from heaven like the rush of a mighty wind, and it filled all the house where they were sitting.

—Acts 2:1-2

T H E   P E N T A G O N, standing in Arlington, Virginia, on the fringe of our nation's capital, is one of the largest and most famous buildings in the world. Lieutenant General Brehan Sommerville pushed through the completion of this amazing five-faced, five-story building in sixteenth months. Many caustic and humorous remarks were made during and immediately following its construction. Some referred to it as "Sommerville's folly." Among the stories was that of the Western Union boy who went in the Pentagon to deliver a message, got lost, and finally emerged a colonel.

This "city in itself" covers about forty-two acres of ground. It originally represented an expenditure of approximately $100,000,000. The inconceivable dimensions of the huge building are even more impressive when one is reminded that the Queen Mary, Empire State Building and the Washington Monument could all be housed within its walls. The Pentagon contains thirty-four acres of floor space which is fifty per cent more than Chicago's famed Merchandise Mart. During office hours it is occupied by about 100,000 people. There are seventeen and one-half miles of corridors in this unique structure. There are one hundred twenty acres of lawn to cut. Despite its enormous size, the Pentagon is said to be exceedingly well managed. Its two hundred telephone operators handle 350,000 calls a day. Some 55,000 people are fed in its cafeterias daily. From ten to twelve tons of waste paper is salvaged every twenty-four hours.[1]

Defense of the Western world is planned and patroled from the Pentagon. It is an intricate and guarded communications center through which thousands of secret dispatches and directives are sent to our troops and top government officials day and night. Thus the Pentagon is far more than an incomprehensible building housing personnel; it has become a symbol of world power. There are those who fear lest it should become America's "golden calf"—the object of supreme loyalty and the altar of total sacrifice.

There is an enormous contrast between the pretentiousness of the Pentagon and that anonymous place in Jerusalem where early believers waited for the visitation of the Spirit! The Pentagon speaks of preparedness and physical power. Pentecost speaks of personal propagation and spiritual power. The Pentagon is primarily identified with the strength and well-being of America. Pentecost speaks of the transforming and Saving Person of Galilee who came that the world might have life.

Although the philosophy of the Pentagon and the philosophy of Pentecost are not diametrically opposed to one another, they nevertheless represent different and sometimes conflicting concepts of sovereignty. The Pentagon represents defense;

[1]See *The Saturday Evening Post,* October 16, 1943; *Fortune Magazine,* April, 1945; *American Magazine,* January, 1951; *Holiday,* March, 1952.

Pentecost the ultimate destiny of man. One majors in protection, while the other majors in the propagation of the gospel of Jesus Christ.

Today is Pentecost. What does it mean? Literally speaking, it means "fiftieth." Originally it was a great event in the Jewish calendar which marked the day their forefathers came to Mt. Sinai. It was also celebrated as the Feast of the Harvest. Coming fifty days after Easter in the Christian calender it is remembered as the day of the visitation of the Holy Spirit.

For a striking account of what transpired we turn to the Book of Acts. In the first chapter we read, " 'But you shall receive power when the Holy Spirit has come upon you; and you shall be my witnesses in Jerusalem and in all Judea and Samaria and to the end of the earth.' " (Acts 1:8.) Jesus promised his followers the power that would enable them to overcome the enslaving sins of their culture and prepare them for more adequate demonstrations of their faith. Without Spirit-given power, there can be no Pentecost.

Furthermore, the early Christians had the faith to believe they would receive this power. "When the day of Pentecost had come, they were all together in one place. And suddenly a sound came from heaven like the rush of a mighty wind, and it filled all the house where they were sitting." They were frightened, yet they were wonderfully empowered to speak. The worshipers had moved beyond curiosity to total commitment to Christ. Simon Peter, with all his imperfections, found himself preaching with new and convincing power. The church came into visible view. The community of faith was established and some three thousand souls were added to the fellowship.

Ours is a day of inconceivable power. Nations are poised, ready to strike. Groups of people within a given country are politically, racially, and socially organized to demand their rights. Science has ushered in a new age of power and fear. In this day when life is endangered by fallouts, it would seem that we are more interested in physical preservation than in moral righteousness and spiritual integrity. Are we not more concerned over the possibilities of outer space than over the predicament of mankind?

The present armament race should convince us that external power results in conflict. This is our dilemma: the world is packed with power yet there is no peace. Jesus not only promised power, he bequeathed peace: " 'Peace I leave with you; my peace I give to you; not as the world gives do I give to you. Let not your hearts be troubled, neither let them be afraid.' " (John 14:27.)

Looking over a heterogeneous band of followers, recalling their problems and anticipating their temptations, of all available gifts Jesus gave them peace—a peace that came from the saving experience of God's presence and love. His peace is the essence of integrity, truth, forgiveness, and love. The legacy of Christ is not conflict, but peace.

A strange, yet satisfying, peace prevailed at Pentecost. Though frightened, the early witnesses experienced a deep and animating peace. They were compelled to share the Good News. "Woe to me if I do not preach the gospel!" (1 Corinthians 9:16.)

One cannot hope even vaguely to comprehend Pentecost without understanding the word "spirit." The dictionary defines spirit as "the breath of life." Breath is the quality and sign of life and without it the body is dead. According to the Genesis story of creation God "breathed into his nostrils the breath of life; and man became a living being." (Genesis 2:7.)

On the day of Pentecost, God breathed new life into his emerging church and believers spoke with flaming tongues. It was a new creation.

Another equally important phenomenon is that the spirit of life is contagious. Whereas God initiates life, man can transfer it. Physically speaking, of course, it is possible to restore breath to the body. But even more significant, individuals have a way of radiating influence. Personality is contagious and persuasive. Pessimism and optimism are optional attitudes; each of us chooses our witness. A leader is a person who is able to transfer his spirit to others. It is said that Toscanini had the rare ability of infusing his orchestra with a spirit and intensity that enabled them to perform at near perfection. Chotzinoff said of Toscanini, "He did not exercise power, he radiated it." There is no power comparable to the strength of the Spirit. Jesus demonstrated this to a degree we shall never fully comprehend. But we know the security of love, the comfort of truth, and the contagion of faith.

Pentecost reassures us of the power and presence of the Holy Spirit. The disciples were first to discover this strange power. They felt it when they were with Jesus. They were encouraged and strengthened for their tasks. After Jesus had gone, they were perplexed. Then one day as they were together in fellowship at Jerusalem recalling his teachings and abiding in prayer, they were aware of the Presence. God's Spirit burned with new intensity upon the altars of their hearts.

The Holy Spirit clarifies our memory of what the Lord said and did. It alerts us to the guidance of God. The Holy Spirit is the continuing presence and power of God making himself known in the church through Christ. Even as the early disciples waited with expectancy and with intense concentration, so may we receive the Holy Spirit. Nels Ferré says, "The Holy Spirit is God personally present. He is wisdom beyond our keenest thought. He is communication beyond our most penetrating speech."[2] Without the Holy Spirit the church dies.

---

[2]From *The Sun and the Umbrella*, by Nels F. S. Ferré. Copyright 1953 by Harper & Brothers. Used by permission.

Martin Dibelius reminds us, "The Christian communities were witnesses to the new forces. That is, they were witnesses to the Holy Spirit acting in this world as the pledge and instrument of the eternal world."[3] And so must the church today.

What man needs desperately is not the power of nuclear fission, but the power of Christian faith. Pentecostal power is what we crave. But only when we fulfill the conditions of Pentecost will we experience the power.

When Charles Tudor Leber was speaking in Sao Paulo, Brazil, his interpreter was a genial American and president of a college in Brazil. The educator was a scholar of the Portuguese language. At his climax Dr. Leber spontaneously said, "Not by might, nor by power, but by my Spirit, says the Lord of hosts." His interpreter hesitated. Dr. Leber repeated the sentence of Scripture. After an embarrassing pause, the educator whispered, "I'm sorry, friend, I've fogotten how to translate that." Informally the interpreter turned to the audience and asked if anyone could translate the sentence. Finally, Dr. Leber continued. After his address, a boy shyly pushed his way through the crowd, holding in his hand an open book and proudly pointed to the place, exclaiming in broken English, "Here it is, mister! Here it is, mister!"[4] The lad had found the passage in his Portuguese Bible.

Certainly this is the paradox of our age. We are possessors of vast information and have access to tremendous power, but somehow we have forgotten how to translate the truth, "Not by might, nor by power, but by my Spirit, says the Lord of hosts." (Zechariah 4:6.)

Pentecost bears testimony to the power of prayer. Ten days of prayer preceded Pentecost. The one hundred twenty waited in meditation and in hope. Let no one underestimate the

---

[3]From *The Sermon on the Mount.* Copyright 1940 by Charles Scribner's Sons.
[4]From *Is God in There?* by Charles Tudor Leber. Copyright, 1948, by Fleming H. Revell Company. Used by permission.

power of prayer. "Prayer," says Dr. Ferré, "is personal communication with God. Prayer is man's real relation to God in
the Spirit."[5] May the church never misuse nor misplace her
prayers. The question is not: Will God answer our prayer?
but: What if he should?

William Booth, founder of the Salvation Army, was converted in Wesleyan Chapel, Nottingham, England. A plaque
marks the spot where this noble friend of the friendless received his spiritual baptism. Through the years leaders of the
Salvation Army have journeyed to the historic shrine in search
of inspiration. One day an elderly Negro, dressed in the simple
uniform of a street preacher, was found by the minister of
the chapel, standing quietly gazing at the memorial to General Booth. When the visitor saw the host pastor, he asked,
"Can a man say his prayers here?" "Of course!" was the reply.
Whereupon he immediately went to his knees. With folded
hands and uplifted head he was heard to pray, "Oh, God, do
it again; do it again!"

This sincere and searching prayer is pertinent at Pentecost.
Under God, Christians must perpetuate the miracles of Pentecost. As we humbly enter the sanctuary of our better selves,
as we recall the ancient promise of power, the visitation of the
Holy Spirit, let us all pray, "Dear God, do it again—and do
it through me!"

[5]Ferré, *op. cit.*

How Much Is Enough?

Thanks be to God for his inexpressible gift!
—2 Corinthians 9:15

THIS DECLARATION reveals Paul's consuming sense of gratitude to Almighty God for his supreme gift in Christ. Out of this consciousness he wrote the church at Corinth concerning its contributions to the needy Christians in Jerusalem. Paul was interested in the solidarity of the church and took the initiative in gathering love offerings.

In his message to the Corinthians the apostle reminded them that if they sowed sparingly they would also reap sparingly. (2 Corinthians 9:6.) Liberality, he maintained, was an indication of one's acceptance of the gospel. As he contemplated the generosity, mercy, and goodness of God, it seemed redundant to urge Christians to give. He reasoned it was only necessary to remind them of the channels through which they might express their love.

Paul's motivation was not political, neither was he trying to make an impression. He wrote as a fellow servant and sufferer. What kind of man was this who asked the Corinthian church to give so liberally? He did not write out of expediency or desire of self-gain. His entire life was a witness to his gratitude for God's gift in Christ and his love of all the churches. These are his words:

Five times I have received at the hands of the Jews the forty lashes less one. Three times I have been beaten with rods; once I was stoned. Three times I have been shipwrecked; a night and a day I have been adrift at sea; on frequent journeys, in danger from rivers, danger from robbers, danger from my own people, danger from Gentiles, danger in the city, danger in the wilderness, danger at sea, danger from false brethren; in toil and hardship, through many a sleepless night, in hunger and thirst, often without food, in cold and exposure. And, apart from other things, there is the daily pressure upon me of my anxiety for all the churches. (2 Corinthians 11:24-28.)

This is the man who said, "Thanks be to God for his inexpressible gift."

The New Testament is saturated with the thought of Christ as God's gift to men. Indeed, it is the good news. "God so loved the world that he gave his only Son, that whoever believes in him should not perish but have eternal life." (John 3:16.)

"He who did not spare his own Son but gave him up for us all, will he not also give us all things with him?" (Romans 8:32.)

Moreover, life itself is a precious and irreplaceable gift. Even goodness and faith are gifts of God's grace. When we recall our blessings, his mysterious yet personal providence, the promise of eternal life, we realize more fully than ever the unanswerable words, "For what can a man give in return for his life?" (Mark 8:37.)

Confronted by the graciousness of God one cannot help but ask himself searching questions:

How much bargaining is enough? Perhaps we should face still other queries. What does the church mean to you? Is it just a nice, though tattered, religious tradition we are seeking to preserve? Is it simply a meeting place for people who look alike, think alike, and act alike? Or is it the "home of the soul" —the Christian community organized for action and redemption? Has the church cost you enough for you to honor it?

There is an arresting story in 1 Chronicles. It concerns David the king. He contemplated the building of an altar to his God. He was interested in a piece of ground owned by Ornan, a Jebusite, as a possible site for the temple in Jerusalem. The king approached Ornan to purchase the property. When the owner of the land learned of David's desire, he generously offered to give it. Furthermore he volunteered oxen for the sacrifice and wood for the fire. But the king refused Ornan's gift saying, "No, but I will buy it for the full price; I will not take for the Lord what is yours, nor offer burnt offerings which cost me nothing." (1 Chronicles 21:24.)

David feared a bargain. He knew all too well that no one could afford to compromise his religious concerns and convictions. The investment and sacrifice of another man could not satisfy his own accountable stewardship.

How much restitution is enough? This query reminds me of a former parishioner who at a rather advanced age accepted Christ and identified himself with the church. He became an admirable churchman. He was exceedingly generous. I once commented on it, to which he replied, "I have a lot of catching up to do." And so do we all.

In varying degrees, we permit pleasures, business and personal plans to take precedence over commitments to the church. While attempting to get ahead in the world, we sometimes get behind in our obligations to the church. This is a continuing and condemning paradox of professing Christians.

Zacchaeus is a study in restitution. He was the chief publican of Jericho. He apparently accumulated his wealth by squeezing and sweating small operators. Zacchaeus was a hard and merciless tax collector, yet he was insecure. Having heard of the strange Galilean who roamed the country preaching a new gospel, and learning of his presence in Jericho, Zacchaeus desired to see Jesus. Being too small and light to push his way through the gathering crowd, he ran ahead, climbed a tree and waited for the Master.

Apparently our observing Lord saw him first, for he said, " 'Zacchaeus, make haste and come down, for I must stay at your house today.' " (Luke 19:5.)

The man, short in stature and shorter in principle, scurried down the tree. The astonished people complained that the Lord would dine with such a notorious sinner. All the while Zacchaeus was accepting a new way of life and presently announced, " 'Lord, the half of my goods I give to the poor; and if I have defrauded any one of anything, I restore it fourfold.' " (Luke 19:8.)

Not only did he make a sincere confession but even more— he was willing to make restitution. To this man Jesus said, " 'Today salvation has come to this house. . .' " (Luke 19:9.)

Imagining this conversation, Lloyd C. Douglas wrote:

"Zacchaeus," said the carpenter gently, "what did you see that made you desire this peace?"

"Good master, I saw—mirrored in your eyes—the face of the Zacchaeus I was meant to be."[1]

This transforming power is the continuing miracle. May each one of us see in Jesus the person he would have us be and, by his grace, strive to become.

How much tithing is enough? From time immemorial man has endeavored to discover the meaning of life and his obli-

---

[1]From "The Mirror," by Lloyd C. Douglas from *The American Pulpit Series.* Used by permission of Abingdon Press.

gations. Gradually tithing emerged as a tangible means of acknowledging and paying one's debts to God. Where it first emerged no one knows. Bishop Costen J. Harrell says in *Stewardship and the Tithe,* "The idea of the tithe did not originate with the Jews." Long before the Old Testament was written, the Chaldeans, Egyptians, Carthaginians, Phoenicians, Greeks, and Romans employed some form of tithing. The rise of this institution is both fascinating and humbling.

Ancient Hebrews practiced tithing with regularity. It was a part of their law and their faith. It involved far more than money and taxes. It frequently demanded the first of their fruits and flocks and families.

Tithing is not a barter with God. It is not a financial contract that assures the participant an increase in profits if he commits himself to tithe. Neither is it a mathematical formula for placating the wrath of God, nor a clever device for lining the coffers of the church. Tithing is essentially a testimony to faith in the creativity and goodness of God. It is an adventure of faith. Thus our gratitude becomes planned giving. It is proportionate giving. It is intelligent giving. It is grateful giving.

Jesus did not destroy the tithe, nor the ancient law. He excelled them. The tithe was the normal stewardship standard of the Old Testament. The background of man's giving is always God's giving. The cross looms as the ultimate in Christian love and faith.

How much of your tithe should be given to the church? The majority of it. Certainly one cannot tithe what he does not have. Tithing should never be considered the ceiling, only the floor, in financing one's faith. Tithing to some would be difficult while to others it would be far too easy. However, it is an equitable starting point in our pilgrimage of faith.

How much devotion is enough? The Christian must constantly examine himself at the point of his loyalty to the Lord. He must not only inventory himself, but demonstrate his love. Definitions of Christianity will not long suffice, only contagious demonstrations will satisfy.

During the last week of our Lord's earthly ministry, he visited in Bethany. While having supper with friends in the home of Simon the leper, a woman, perhaps from the streets, shyly entered the shadowy room and anointed the Master's head with "pure nard." It was costly. Speedily the perfume pervaded the air and quickly came criticism and comment. To many it was sheer waste. Some of the self-righteous observers reminded the Lord that the vial of ointment could have been sold for "'more than three hundred denarii, and given to the poor.'" But Jesus lauded the woman, saying, "'Let her alone; why do you trouble her? She has done a beautiful thing to me.'" (Mark 14:5-6.)

Why was it beautiful? Because her love was lifted to the level of extravagance. The hope Jesus gave her was overwhelming. She desired above all to assure the Lord of her complete devotion. The economy of duty suddenly became the beautiful extravagance of enduring love.

How much prayer is enough? Jesus declared that men "ought always to pray and not lose heart." (Luke 18:1.)

Prayer is not a mechanical device for tuning in on outer space. It is a means of spiritual communication. Prayer is far more than petitioning God for our wants. It is being still long enough to want God. Prayer is communion. It is fellowship. It lends perspective. Prayer brings peace. Prayer leads to power. A careful reading of the life of Jesus reveals the frequency of his praying. He was a man of prayer.

How often do you pray for your church?

We are told that Brother Lawrence spent ten years learning how to pray. Friedrich Heiler says,

Belief in God's personality and the assurance of His presence are the two presuppositions of prayer. But prayer itself is no mere belief in the reality of a personal God—such a belief underlies even a theistic metaphysic;—nor is it a mere experience of His presence—for this is the accompaniment of the entire life and thought of the great men of religion. Prayer is rather a living relation of man to God, a direct and inner contact, a refuge, a mutual intercourse, a conversation, spiritual commerce, an association, a fellowship, a communion, a converse, a one-ness, a union of an "I" and a "Thou."[2]

If we would discover the deeper satisfactions of the Christian life, we must learn the disciplines of prayer. John Marshall of Virginia was a churchman. Under his leadership for the first time the Supreme Court became an effective instrument of justice. Like the Apostle Paul, he, too, was acquainted with "fighting without and fear within." (2 Corinthians 7:5.) Through it all, he was able to maintain a wonderful equilibrium. Marshall's concept of constitutional law emanated from his concept of God. After his wife's death he formed the habit of spending a portion of each Sunday afternoon reading aloud the church service for that day as though she were at his side. John Marshall knew that a life devoted to public service and justice demanded a life of prayer.

How much service is enough? The Christian is warned that the day comes when he can no longer work. Sincere followers of Christ have always been hard-working, energetic souls who believed their daily contributions to the kingdom were of enduring worth.

Think of Polycarp, Bishop of Smyrna, who at the age of eighty-six was dragged into an arena to renounce his faith or

2From *Prayer*, by Friedrich Heiler. Copyright 1932 by Oxford University Press. Used by permission.

be destroyed. Who ever heard of a man eighty-six giving a community trouble? He did. "But when the Pro-Consul pressed him and said: 'Take the oath and I let you go, revile Christ,' Polycarp said: 'For eighty and six years have I been his servant, and he has done me no wrong, and how can I blaspheme my King who saved me?' "[3]

The saintly bishop chose to be burned at the stake rather than speak one word against Jesus Christ.

We cannot forget John Wesley who preached effectively until he was more than eighty; who traveled five thousand miles a year and mostly on horseback. He preached approximately fifteen sermons a week.

Consider Albert Schweitzer, a four-star general of the cross, who is regarded as the world's greatest living man and one of the great souls of all time, who continues to perform miracles in Lambarene, Africa. He is many years beyond normal retirement. When an interviewer asked him to comment on his sacrifice, he said, "I cannot speak on sacrifice because I know nothing about it."

How much money is enough for the Lord? Money talks. It says many things to many people. It also speaks of one's love for Christ.

Ours is a most prosperous and mercenary period. Values are so distorted that today's bankers may be the first in history to go broke with their banks full of money. Savings are at an all-time high. Per capita income is unexcelled. Despite unprecedented financial campaigns and increased giving to religious work, we are advised that Protestants have lost ground in their giving. We have not kept pace with inflation nor with personal prosperity. For instance, in 1931 the per capita income of Americans was $439, yet the per capita gift was

---

[3]From *Apostolic Fathers II*, translated by Kirsopp Lake. Copyright 1913, The Loeb Classical Library and Harvard University Press. Used by permission.

$19.89, representing a gift of 4.53 per cent. Twenty-five years later in 1956, our per capita income had increased to $1,940, with per capita giving amounting to $53.94, or 2.77 per cent.[4]

What is happening to America? What is happening to professing Christians? Do we place comforts before Christ?

Edward K. Ziegler has most aptly described our days for many in these facetious and frightening lines:

> Science is my shepherd; I shall not want.
> He maketh me to lie down on foam-rubber mattresses;
> He leadeth me beside the six-lane highways.
> He rejuvenateth my thyroid glands;
> He leadeth me in the paths of psychoanalysis
>   for peace of mind's sake.
> Yea, though I walk through the valley of the shadow
>   of the Iron Curtain, I will fear no communist,
> for thou art with me; and thy radar screen, thy
>   *hydrogen bomb,* they comfort me.
> Thou preparest a banquet before me in the presence
>   of the world's billion hungry people;
> Thou anointest my head with home permanents;
>   my beer glass foameth over.
> Surely prosperity and pleasure shall follow me
>   all the days of my life,
> and I shall dwell in Shangri-La forever.[5]

Once again let us turn the pages of our New Testament for an insight into gratitude and generosity. Our Lord sat with his disciples over against the treasury of the temple. The ancient money box was in full view. A colorful crowd inched its way past the depository. Many were the gifts. However, lives and not gifts were in the balance. Presently a poor widow shyly threaded her way through the multitude. Unobtrusively

---

[4]See *Stewardship Facts,* Arthur O. Rinden, Editor, published by the Department of Stewardship and Benevolence, National Council of Churches of Christ in the U. S. A., 257 Fourth Avenue, New York 10, N. Y., 1957, p. 49.

[5]"The Materialist's Twenty-third Psalm," by Edward K. Ziegler. Used by permission of the author.

she dropped two copper coins into the treasury. Jesus saw her and was tremendously moved. "And he said, 'Truly I tell you, this poor widow has put in more than all of them; for they all contributed out of their abundance, but she out of her poverty put in all the living that she had.'" (Luke 21:3-4.)

The anonymous and ever-haunting woman gave out of gratitude and love. Faith had taken the initiative. In *Twelve Baskets Full,* Margaret T. Applegarth refers to the widow's example as "the little woman who started this big Mite Box Movement."

There should be an element of sacrifice in one's gift to the church. Roy O. McClain maintains that there can be no worship without sacrifice:

> When no sacrifice is remembered in advance, the worshiper comes with the "What can I get out of it?" attitude instead of "What can I put into it?" No verb so impedes the art of effectual worship as does the verb "to get." It is true that in some situations there is little or nothing to get; but there is also the fact that some professing Christians have nothing to take it away in had there been anything there to get![6]

However, the history of the race indicates that sacrifice has never been pleasant nor easy. Yet our Bible is suffused with the message of sacrifice. Jesus continues to survey his church.

During a Sunday morning worship service in our sanctuary, a child wrote some notes. Among them was a brief message to God. The card was placed in an offering envelope which eventually reached me. It read, "Dear God, I love you. Do you love me? Answer yes."

Today you are asked to write God a message on a pledge card. Write it in such a way that he will know how much you love him.

---

[6]From *This Way, Please,* by Roy O. McClain. Copyright 1957 by Fleming H. Revell Company. Used by permission.

The Challenge of The Church

"Go therefore and make disciples of all nations, bap-
tizing them in the name of the Father and of the Son
and of the Holy Spirit, teaching them to observe all
that I have commanded you; and lo, I am with you
always, to the close of the age."

—*Matthew 28:19-20*

T H E   C H U R C H is not a Riviera resort for the redeemed. It is, as Charles Clayton Morrison says, "a society of sinners." The church is not a success club, nor an amusement center, nor is it a convenient drive-in where we honk for service; neither is it a supermarket in which we bump carts with our neighbors. The church is not a public forum designed to attract the intelligentsia and other celebrities of the community. The church is always more than you see.

Richard Niebuhr says the institutional church is no more the kingdom of God than natural science is nature. Imposing buildings and impressive statistics are not synonymous with the kingdom. Emil Brunner warns that we must never confuse the visible with the invisible church, nor mistake its organization for its fellowship. Whatever else the church may be, it is the Christian community, the family of forgiveness, God's trustee on earth until his kingdom comes.

Bishop Austin Pardue says the church is the "communion of saints." Lest he should become archaic in his definition of a saint he quickly adds, "a saint is anyone who is trying to practice the faith." Theodore O. Wedel of Washington refers to the church as "the colony of heaven." Certainly nothing on this earth is more heavenly in its dimensions and dedication than the true church of Jesus Christ. It is the continuing testimony of the Lord. The church is the Christian community in action. Christians are not those who have arrived and who are totally satisfied with their spiritual sensitivity and maturity, but they are people who are seeking the way to the city whose builder and keeper is God. Being pilgrims, they are not perfect, but they long to know more intimately the perfect One.

One of the things that influenced Harry Emerson Fosdick in his younger days to shift from teaching to the preaching ministry was the challenge of the church. Early he saw it as the carrier of the Christian faith from one generation to another and "the mother of all Christians."

The church then is visible and invisible, measurable and mysterious, local and universal. What is its challenge? Many get along without it, while some are apparently miserable in it. However, its mission is precisely the same as it was when our Lord walked this earth, namely, to turn the hearts, thoughts, and wills of men toward God.

The continuing challenge of the church is to imitate Jesus Christ. In writing to the Philippians, Paul said, "Have this mind among yourselves, which you have in Christ Jesus, who, though he was in the form of God, did not count equality with God a thing to be grasped, but emptied himself, taking the form of a servant, being born in the likeness of men." (Philippians 2:5-8.) Do we seriously strive to imitate our Lord or do we prefer to practice the conduct of our superiors and admirers? In the delicate dimension of dignified neutrality critics often observe the insincerity of Christians.

The late Peter Marshall maintained that one of the reasons why the church fails to attract and hold people is that its members enjoy sinning too much to be Christian and are too Christian to enjoy sinning.

Followers of Jesus are expected to practice his teachings—to embody in themselves his good will, his gentleness, his understanding, and his generous mercy. Membership in the church is not synonymous with the Christian life. A lady once asked me, "How long does one have to belong to the church before he is Christian?"

There were few marginal members in the early fellowship. First-century Christians felt personally responsible for propagating the faith. Only the strong of heart and body survived. The expansion of Christianity was a costly crusade. The early Christians knew in whom they believed.

A stranger visiting a Methodist community in Britain asked an old Cornishman to explain the obvious morality and spirit of the villagers. He replied, "A man named Wesley passed this way." And so must the church of Jesus Christ constantly remind the observing world that Jesus of Nazareth is passing by. There is an irresistible contagion about the Christian.

The challenge of the church is to demonstrate fellowship. It is a familiar word but perhaps we should review what Webster says about it: "Fellowship is the companionship of persons on equal and friendly terms. . .; a union, or association; partnership. . .;—*v.i.* to be in a communion with the church."

There is a unique beauty and distinction about a congregation. However heterogeneous, there is a harmony of purpose. No other group shares such genuine concern for people. There is an intimacy and trustfulness in a church found only in a Christian family. The church is God's way of linking life with life, love with love, and hope with heaven.

I was privileged to be sent on a trip around the world by a congregation I once served. From that memorable experience I gained many new insights into the meaning of the church. Before my departure officers of our congregation assembled in the chapel for worship, the climax of which was the celebration of the Lord's Supper. Subsequently, they followed my itinerary and remembered me in prayer, even as I did the congregation.

Soon I was to discover that the intimacy and trustfulness of the local fellowship also characterizes the larger fellowship. For instance, at our mission station, Pendra Road, India, our arrival was celebrated by a special program in the village church. Nor shall I soon forget the evening that a stranger approached me at the airport in the Fiji Islands and invited me to spend the night with him, assuring me that he was Christian—a Methodist—even as was his entire family. The inclusiveness of the fellowship of Christ is the miracle of transforming love.

John Oxenham understood this when he wrote:

> In Christ there is no East or West,
> In Him no South or North:
> But one great fellowship of love
> Throughout the whole wide earth.[1]

The challenge of the church is to demonstrate Christian concern for individuals and their society. Churchmen are expected to be heralds of the good news that God lives and that Christ is available. The early church had a passion for people. They not only believed that Jesus came to seek and to save the lost, but also felt impelled to walk the roads of their community and to search out the forgotten. The common cry

---

[1] From *Bees in Amber*. Used by permission of the American Tract Society.

was: " 'Repent, and be baptized every one of you in the name of Jesus Christ for the forgiveness of your sins; and you shall receive the gift of the Holy Spirit.' " (Acts 2:38.)

Many are the evidences of increased interest in the church. We are witnessing a revival in evangelism. As in the first century, even so today, the fields are white unto the harvest but the laborers are all too few. Ours is a changing America. Great and sudden shifts in population challenge the church with new problems and possibilities. We have today more than 171,000,000 people in our country. The population is increasing at the rate of 7,500 a day. Statisticians estimate that by 1975, the population of the United States will have increased to more than 220,000,000. According to Jesse M. Bader, 60.9 per cent is the highest percentage of the country's population ever reported as belonging to a religious group or denomination.[2] Who will house, feed, and church these people?

Even as the Saving Person of Galilee was impartial and all-inclusive in his concern for people, so must be the church today. The Great Commission is all-inclusive.

Leslie D. Weatherhead in *That Immortal Sea* tells of a fine young man who prepared for the mission field and awaited appointment. While out walking one day beside a canal, he saw a boy fall in. The young man plunged into the water and rescued the lad. Something happened in the struggle and the cleric lost his life. Later it was discovered that the lad whom he saved from drowning was none other than the village idiot, whom many thought was a burden to his family and society. But, as Dr. Weatherhead emphasized, nobody said it was silly of the young missionary to bother. Rather everyone was impressed that a man so brilliant, so promising, would freely and spontaneously give himself for another.

---

[2]See *Evangelism in a Changing America,* by Jesse M. Bader.   Copyright 1957 by Bethany Press.

In some such way, the church challenges its members to demonstrate the genuineness of God. Love is courageous. Jesus laid down his life for all types and conditions of men. The cross is integrated and is a universal reminder of the miracle of love. As a member of the church, through your unique and unrepeatable life you are to bear a contagious witness for Christ where you live.

The challenge of the church is to demonstrate "suffering love." ". . . Christ loved the church and gave himself up for her, that he might sanctify her, having cleansed her by the washing of water with the word, . . ." (Ephesians 5:25-26.) The church possesses a dimension of depth and compassion that knows no boundaries. Jesus demonstrated it again and again in his ministry. Without suffering love, there can be no church.

In *Triumph over Tragedy*, Iona Henry tells of the anguish experienced when she and her husband lost their only daughter, Jane, who was in her early teens. Mrs. Henry speaks of their bitterness and resentfulness. Then a few weeks later, near Granite City, Illinois, while en route to Wichita, Kansas, their car was struck by a train. Her husband and ten-year-old son were killed instantly. She was hospitalized for more than one hundred days. Her description of how her friends in Chatham, New Jersey, surrounded her with love, messages of encouragement, the call of her family physician, and a visit from her pastor who was sent at the cost of the community, is a beautiful story of suffering love. In its pages we see the strong soul of Iona Henry emerging through lonely and painful struggle to a new determination and dedication. She turned back to school and today she is teaching in a university. Mrs. Henry concludes her testimony with this sentence: "For I have walked far in the valleys of the unknown land, and I have come safely through."[3]

The challenge of the church is to be perfect. " 'You, therefore, must be perfect, as your heavenly Father is perfect.' " (Matthew 5:48.)

Scholars remind us that Jesus is not here challenging us to be perfect in the sense of being flawless, impeccable, and without stain. "Instead," says Roy Pearson, "we are to be perfect in the sense that we aim at perfection, that we judge our lives in terms of him who alone is perfect, that we imitate God in all we think and say and do."[4]

People have a way of saying: "It is good enough. Leave it alone. Let sleeping dogs lie." Unlike the good Samaritan, these are expressions of neutral, noncommitted persons, who would rather get by than get involved in situations that require Christian courage and costly expenditure. The fashioners of history have been diligent and extravagant people who believed in perfection.

Tennyson is said to have altered every line of his famous poem, *In Memoriam.*

Chopin would shut himself up in his room for days, weeping, walking the floor, breaking pencils, repeating and altering a bar of music as often as a hundred times. It was not uncommon for him to spend six weeks on a single page of copy.

Harry Emerson Fosdick will go down in history as one of the great preachers of all times. A brilliant student who never took anything for granted, he set for himself the high standard of one hour's preparation for each minute of preaching.

---

[3]From *Triumph over Tragedy,* by Iona Henry with Frank S. Mead. Copyright 1957 by Fleming H. Revell Company. Used by permission.

[4]From *The Hard Commands of Jesus,* by Roy Pearson. Copyright 1957 by Abingdon Press. Used by permission.

Consider one of the most honored writers of our day, Ernest Hemingway. He is an unusually disciplined stylist. One has only to read his Nobel-prize-winning *The Old Man and the Sea* to glimpse his passion for perfection. Every sentence is carefully manicured and the story moves with suspense.

The challenge of the church is for its members to strive for perfection in every action and expression of life, knowing all too well that their finest efforts will appear pale in contrast to the One who said, "It is finished."

The challenge of the church is to engage in worship: to ponder on the glory of God, to join in congregational prayers, to offer and seek forgiveness, to confess one's sins and to re-commit one's self to his church, to sing the hymns of faith, to expose one's soul to the highest. " 'For where two or three are gathered in my name,' " said Jesus, " 'there am I in the midst of them.' " (Matthew 18:20.)

Worship is the supreme venture of the Christian. The extending of his soul to God is the therapy he seeks and the strength he gains. Every man worships something or somebody. As Theodore Parker said, "If he worships not the true God, he will have his idols."

We are drunk with the wines of our time. Not all drunkenness is from alcohol. We are drunk with noise, novelty, speed, sputnik, and modern living. We scarcely have time to be polite, let alone pray. All too often our work takes precedence over our worship, and the club over the church. Charles B. Templeton has called our day one of "chrome-plated chaos."

Many are our opportunities to worship, but none equals that offered by the church. I shall never forget an experience in North Carolina. I had tried to impress the custodian with the importance of having the church in readiness for budget Sunday. Apparently I oversold him, for at 1:30 A.M. on Victory Sunday, he called to say, "Rev'in, don't worry, the church is ready. . ." Though slightly exasperated at the timing of his call, I nevertheless appreciated his concern. The building was ready; how about the congregation?

Happy are those who anticipate the worship services of their church and who wait in awe for the visitation of the Spirit.

The challenge of the church is to demonstrate its essential oneness. In writing to the Ephesians, Paul said, "There is one body and one Spirit, just as you were called to the one hope that belongs to your call, one Lord, one faith, one baptism, one God and Father of us all, who is above all and through all and in all." (Ephesians 4:4-6.)

The church of Jesus Christ is "essentially, intentionally, and constitutionally one." Our divisions are of men, not of God. The sin of sectarianism is a travesty against the kingdom of God. No communion can boast of possessing or demonstrating the whole truth. Truth is impartial. It makes no difference whether it is spoken by Catholic, Orthodox, Jew, or Protestant. Truth is truth. And only in truth, not interpretations of truth, shall we find the freedom we crave and the unity we seek.

Christians are challenged to rediscover and to demonstrate their God-given togetherness. The ecumenical movements of our day, notably the National and World Councils of Churches, are not pressing for amalgamation, compromise, or surrender. Their goal is a more visible demonstration of the church's oneness.

Both Scripture and society demand a closer co-operation and exchange between religious groups, established churches, and ecumenical movements. The challenge of the church is to implement Jesus' unanswered prayer, "that they may be one." (John 17:11.)

Strangely enough, the church challenges its members to get out of it. Not in the sense of staying away from worship, excusing oneself from responsibilities or becoming disgruntled, but rather the opposite—becoming more involved. The church will never redeem society until its members become the priests of the community, carrying its message into every walk of life every day. John Wesley was correct when he maintained that Christ would never disturb anybody shut up in the church. Each member must carry away the spirit of Christ and bear testimony to his faith. This is precisely our problem and challenge; namely, that of extending the boundaries of the church to include every problem and person in the world.

The great issues of our day are influenced by the church but they are not being settled in the church. Matters of war and peace are not being decided in our churches but by conniving politicians. Questions pertaining to management and labor are not particularly considered a concern of the church. The twin tyrants of our time, liquor and gambling, are not being squarely faced by the church. Integration is not as freely discussed in our churches as on the front steps of county courthouses and state capitols and in the headlines of newspapers. If we are sincere about conquering the world for Christ, let us get out of our "ivory towers" with the message of concern and love for people.

In T. S. Eliot's moving drama, *Murder in the Cathedral*, he depicts some of the tensions and temptations of the twelfth century, even the predicament of the faithful. Archbishop Thomas à Becket finally returns from exile. His enemies pursue him to his cathedral. The bishop's courage and confidence are magnificent. Once in the cathedral, the priests insisted on locking the doors:

> Bar the door. Bar the door.
> The door is barred.
> We are safe. We are safe.

How strangely modern! So many feel they are safe because they hold membership in the church.

Then the archbishop rises to unexcelled eloquence and faith:

Unbar the doors! throw open the doors!
I will not have the house of prayer,
   the church of Christ,
The sanctuary, turned into a fortress.
The Church shall protect her own,
   in her own way, not
As oak and stone; stone and oak decay,
Give no stay, but the Church shall endure.
The church shall be open, even to our enemies.   Open the door![5]

Open wide the doors of your church. Fling open the windows of the sanctuary that the prevailing winds of God may pass through and pervade the community. Enthusiastically tell everyone you meet of the One who said, " 'Go therefore and make disciples of all nations, baptizing them in the name of the Father and of the Son and of the Holy Spirit, teaching them to observe all that I have commanded you; and lo, I am with you always, to the close of the age.' " (Matthew 28: 19-20.)

---

[5]From *Murder in the Cathedral*, by T. S. Eliot, copyright, 1935, by Harcourt, Brace and Company, Inc.

Working With Honor
and Honoring Our Work

—each man's work will become manifest.
—1 Corinthians 3:13

I T W A S E L E V E N o'clock Saturday night. Having covered more than 600 miles that day, we were road weary and sought a place to sleep. In the quiet city of more churches than gasoline stations—Memphis, Tennessee—we inquired about accommodations and were directed to an attractive motor court. Though the hour was late, the manager-owner was in and courteously informed us, "We are filled up and have been since six-thirty." Instead of being curt and disagreeable at the lateness of my inquiry, the friendly man had his secretary telephone several people in an effort to place us for the night. The sixth call was successful.

I was greatly impressed by the general demeanor of the man and engaged him in conversation. Among other things, he said, "I came up the hard way. I have been here twenty-two years. We are now filled practically every night. I could have gone home at six o'clock, but I stayed and have assisted thirty people in finding lodging." Then he straightened his strong short frame to its full height and in a tone of sober sincerity concluded, "Whenever I feel my prosperity and good fortune, I think back on the hard days of this business and I stay around to do someone a favor."

What difference does it make if a man operates a tourist court, tutors delinquent students, serves his state and nation, stands in a pulpit, pilots a plane, plows a field, works in a factory, follows a profession, runs a farm or a household, if he works with honor and honors his work? In *Pippa Passes,* Robert Browning reminds us, "All service ranks the same with God." Professional protocol, vocational advantage, and economic security are never lionized nor exaggerated in the Christian community.

However, Christians are not oblivious to the multiple needs of man, nor are they parasites on society. On the contrary, Christians of all generations have endeavored to distinguish between essentials and nonessentials, wants and needs, temporary and permanent values. The story of man's pilgrimage as recorded in the Scriptures is one of struggle, sacrifice, and service. The Bible might well be defined as a manual for Christian workers, written by workers, for workers, about the unfinished business of the Supreme Workman.

Moses was a herdsman; David was a shepherd; Paul a tentmaker; Luke a physician; Lydia a businesswoman; and Jesus a carpenter. Carey was a cobbler; Beethoven a musician, and George Washington Carver a chemist. God's labor union is all-inclusive and it is concerned with far more than bargaining strategy, hours and wages and economic battering rams. It is compassionately concerned with the nature, needs, and destiny of man.

Labor Day Sunday compels us to face the perennial problems associated with making a living and making a life. Paul's admonition to the Corinthians is altogether pertinent, ". . . . each man's work will become manifest."

Ours is a sensate and sensual society in which the physical is paramount. If Emerson could say of his day, "Things are in the saddle and ride mankind," what would he say of ours? We are usually more impressed by what we see than by what we feel. Our connections appear more valuable than our convictions. We are more inclined to place our trust in economic uncertainties than we are to explore spiritual frontiers. We are so unionized that we are victimized; so efficient that we are indifferent; so highly organized that it is difficult to get anything done; so broad-minded that we scarcely know what we believe and so anxious to keep pace with our neighbors that we are feverishly frustrated. The commercial merchants have mesmerized us.

In such a complex and demanding society stands the Christian. Whatever his work, his supreme vocation is bearing witness to the truth that Jesus Christ is the Son of God and Savior of the world. He believes in the abiding dignity of man and in the eternal integrity of God. Therefore the follower of Christ confidently pursues his work, seeing in it not only a livelihood but also a way of life. Whether delivering milk at the back door, running an office or keeping a home, the Christian serves mankind.

If one is to work with honor and honor his work, he must be happy in what he is doing. Discontented people seldom experience therapy or salvation in their work. The Christian should be a joyous person. This is not to suggest flippancy or insincerity, but the true follower of Christ knows an abiding joy that comes from companionship with the Lord of life.

Jesus was immersed in his work. The author of Hebrews admonishes us to look "to Jesus the pioneer and perfecter of our faith, who for the joy that was set before him endured the cross, despising the shame, and is seated at the right hand of the throne of God." (Hebrews 12:2).

It is good to see a man happy in his work. He will doubt-less whistle or sing as he surveys his tasks with pride and thanksgiving. Such a workman is both creative and produc-tive.

Once while in Richmond, Virginia, I stopped to see my old barber. I not only needed a haircut, but I also wanted to visit my old friend. His shop was in the shadow of the state capitol, which led to an unexpected political exchange. My friend is a politician of unusual experience, having profes-sionally served nine governors. Moreover he is a churchman and when you take his chair he is just as apt to hand you a new book on religion as the daily paper.

During the visit I said, "Steve, when do you take your vacation?" "Oh," he replied, "I haven't had one in twenty years. I don't need one. I get away for a few days now and then, but my work is my life. I enjoy it. I love people. When I finish at the shop at the end of a day, I'm as fresh as when I started. Then too," he added, "my church is my life. All ten of our children, now grown and scattered across the country, are active in the church and that makes me happy."

If one is to work with honor and honor his work, he must possess a sense of vocation. Unless one desires to fully express himself through his work and derives genuine satisfaction from it, he should re-examine his life in reference to his vocation. The pay check should never be pay enough. The compensa-tions of knowledge, skill, and constructive participation in life should always take precedence over pay. If one works only for money, there will come a day when no amount of it will be adequate or will satisfy.

Elton Trueblood has reminded our generation of the de-clining sense of vocation. Current emphasis seems to be on getting ahead rather than getting behind things that count. The average worker is apparently more interested in economic advancement than in moral and spiritual adventure. Ceaseless demands concerning hours and wages, the chasms that all too often exist between management and labor, are rapidly discoloring the horizons of honor, integrity, and pride of workmanship. Both capital and labor must ever seek to reflect a commendable conscience.

The Greek philosopher, Heraclitus, once said, "You can't step in the same river twice." It is never the same. Life is very much like a rolling river. We can never relive a day. Life is forever moving and without a moment's rest. Therefore it behooves us to give a good account of ourselves every moment of every day. Whatever his station, a Christian will strive to give an honest day's work for an honest day's pay. He will work as with a dream possessed, for in the words of Gerald Kennedy, "To be human means to be captured by a dream."

If one is to work with honor and honor his work, he must have a sense of responsibility. Every workman must feel his share of responsibility (and more) if he amounts to anything or accomplishes any worth-while undertaking. No amount of automation can replace the sensitivity and concern of a responsible person.

We are experiencing an appalling apathy toward the acceptance of responsibility. Regretfully we parents notice it in our children, colleagues, companions, and church members. Yet Jesus devoted much time to teaching people to be responsible. However one earns his living, he has not lived until he has accepted worth-while responsibilities. The Christian life demands discipline and dedication.

There appeared a remarkable story in *Look* under the attractive caption "I Fly the President." In this carefully written article, Colonel William Draper declares that worry is his business and President Eisenhower's safety his reward. There are many interesting and intimate precautions taken by

Colonel Draper's thirty-three-man team responsible for the Columbine III, preparatory to, during, and after a flight. Every member of the crew is a specialist and a perfectionist. Aeronautical standards are not sufficiently demanding to satisfy those who fly the President. An oil leak in the Columbine will keep the crew up all night. Usually two tests are considered adequate to check such a repair. Draper takes ten. The thirty-six-year-old pilot is always available. On a trip he sleeps with not one but two alarm clocks. Aircraft Commander Draper says: "People often ask me what it's like to have the responsibility of the President's life in my hands. I think it demands a special dedication. Everyone in the crew down to the newest mechanic must have it."[1]

If one is to honor his work and work with honor, he must have a desire to serve his fellow men. He must be more concerned with making a contribution to life than he is with carving out for himself the most coveted niche in the community. A happy and helpful workman is one who feels that his job is beneficial to mankind and that he is needed in the scheme of things.

" 'I am among you a servant.' "[2] (Luke 22:27.) Our Lord was not an executive but a servant; not a salesman but a servant; not a strategist but a servant. His declaration is haunting, " 'whoever would be great among you must be your servant, and whoever would be first among you must be slave of all.' " (Mark 10:43-44.) We serve God best by serving others. The Christian is challenged to make a place for the Carpenter of Nazareth in the place where he works.

Before the turn of the century there lived in Boston an extraordinary man, a burly fellow, weighing more than 200

---

[1]From *Look Magazine*, August 20, 1957, as told by William Draper to Lawrence Lader. Used by permission.

[2]From *The Holy Bible: A New Translation*, by James A. Moffatt. Copyright 1922, 1935 and 1950 by Harper & Brothers. Used by permission.

pounds, whose face was as strongly hewn as was his family tree. He was anything but a "Beau Brummel." His attire was frequently unbecoming and his bearded face was not photogenic. His speech was shot through with grammatical errors for he had never finished the eighth grade. He was a clerk in a shoe store.

Once this virtually unknown salesman sat listening to Henry Varley speak and among other challenging statements the preacher declared: "The world yet waits to see what God can do with a man who will dedicate his entire life to him." The preacher hit home. The unlettered man bowed his head and prayed, "God, I will be that man."

Immediately Dwight L. Moody acted. He gave himself to boys' work; taught a Sunday school class; and made himself available to people. Eventually he toured America and Great Britain as a persuasive evangelist—many say the greatest since the Apostle Paul.

Whatever your place in society, tend it with care. Through it your worship is unmistakable and your witness unending.

Why Go to College?

Do your best to present yourself to God as one approved, a workman who has no need to be ashamed, rightly handling the word of truth.

—2 Timothy 2:15

EDUCATION IS our heritage and hope. In 1830 there were only thirty-eight schools of higher learning in America. Today there are some 2,000 colleges and universities, a number equaling the combined total of similar institutions throughout the world.

Even though we are propagating our colonial heritage in education in an unprecedented fashion, the fact remains we are not producing a sufficient number of qualified men and women to man the strategic posts of leadership and learning.

Though college population has increased ten times since the turn of the century, sixty per cent of American citizens over twenty-five years of age have only an eighth-grade education, fourteen per cent have less than five years of schooling, twenty-nine per cent have attended high school (not all graduated), and only eleven per cent of our citizens have college or university degrees.[1]

---

[1] See *Public Affairs Bulletin,* No. 249, "So You Didn't Go to College," by Jerry Klein and Bill Fisher, Jr.

Should you ask the average person how best to solve our common problems, the chances are he would say, "We have to teach people how to be better." In other words, education is supposed to solve all our problems.

This is not true. Many are the baffling paradoxes of our culture. With all of our emphasis on education, we are slow in learning many things. Americans spend more than $10,000,000 a year on alcohol and between $17,000,000 and $25,000,000 in gambling. Juvenile delinquency represents an expenditure of $175,000,000 to $200,000,000 annually, not to mention the staggering cost of crime in general. Forty thousand Americans are killed on our highways every year. The late Dr. Kinsey reported that ninety-eight per cent of American boys who go only through grade school, eighty-four per cent of those who do not exceed high school, and sixty-seven per cent of those who go to college, engage in premarital sex relations.[2] In a society where only about sixty per cent of its citizens proclaim a religious faith and with fewer still practicing what they profess, the critic might well ask, "Does education pay?"

Fred P. Carson in *The Christian Imprint* reports that sixty per cent of the youth of grammar school age, forty per cent of high school age, and twenty per cent of American youth of college age "cannot be called an outstanding success." Have we parents failed? Are the curricula of the schools too far removed from life? Have we expected too much of education? Do we not frequently consider college a success vaccine? Education, says Mark Van Doren, "is a part of life and the part does not direct the whole." Education is not enough in itself, but, given a chance, it will dispel ignorance and prejudice.

Why do you go to college? Just because your parents did, or because they can afford to send you; because it is a popular

[2]See Kinsey, Pomeroy, Martin, *Sexual Behavior in the Human Male,* Philadelphia: W. B. Saunders Company, 1948, p. 552.

thing to do, or because you have an insurance policy which cannot be cashed any other way? College attendance is a happy, serious, and costly business. It affords the opportunity to see life through new prisms. A college degree is not synonymous with intelligence, success, or income. We must cease to believe, indeed if we ever did, that one has to go to college to prepare himself for life or to gain respect. Literally millions of influential and useful men and women never attended college.

David Sarnoff, Russian-born immigrant, formerly a newsboy, chairman of Radio Corporation of America, never went to college. Neither W. K. Kellogg nor Henry J. Kaiser attended college. Charles E. Wilson, former president of General Electric, quit school at the age of twelve to support his mother. Statesman James F. Byrnes and labor leader John L. Lewis did not go to college, nor did Pulitzer-prize-winner Ernest Hemingway, Katharine Cornell, Helen Hayes, or Ethel Barrymore.

College is not a panacea for all our problems, nor does it guarantee prosperity, but it offers unequalled learning opportunities. College is not a must, but it is one of the most important molding forces in our society.

College is not an advanced kindergarten for playboys and -girls, but a seat of learning. I shall never forget an experience on the campus of a great university. A husky lad came up to one of the coaches with whom I was talking and asked him, his advisor, if he would sign the "drop slip" for a certain class. After conference with the so-called student, the coach said to me, "Guess why he wanted to drop the course." I shook my head in the negative. He volunteered, "The course carries a notebook requirement!"

College does not give one a stamp of approval unless the graduate bears the right image.

A fine Indian chief spoke for many college students and graduates when he said he had been through many colleges but none had been through him. It is the scope and quality of one's education, however acquired, that determines his character and contribution to life. To educate a man's mind without conditioning his heart and spirit, maintained Alexander Campbell, is like giving a repeating rifle to a savage.

What then is the challenge of a college education? It is the challenge to accept and make adjustments. In certain areas of life we should be maladjusted. The Christian cannot afford to adjust to the *status quo* and to sin in its many insidious forms. However, some people never learn to adjust at all. They go through life on a tradition or a prejudice.

As parents, one of the most painful responsibilities we carry is that of assisting our children in making intelligent adjustments. This week millions of children and youth will return to school. Some will be going for the first time. Adjustments are demanded of parents and their children. The college campus, be it in the home town or at a distance, is unique in that the student must learn to adjust to a controlled community. He must learn to respect authority, assume responsibility, make decisions, and stand on his own feet. The educated person is one who is able and willing to adjust to his environment. Character is not a crown, but a conquest.

Arnold Toynbee, foremost authority on civilizations of our day, was asked if he felt our Western culture was doomed to perish. Thoughtfully, he replied, "No. In order to endure it has only to fulfill a basic condition, that is, become adjusted to the eternal."

College affords a rare opportunity in the art of making adjustments.

The challenge of a college education is to discover and discipline self. No one can hope to live happily or helpfully until he discovers who he is. Cicero once said, "He who is ignorant of what happened before his birth is always a child." The educated person will be familiar with the species, the sweep of history, and the dangers and satisfactions of living.

As a college counselor, I used to consider it my job to enable that strange student commonly known as a freshman to find himself in the scheme of things. Timidly he would come to me about any number of problems: his classes, his roommate, his girl friend. As counselor it was my responsibility to lead him in a discovery of himself and his relation to others.

Roy A. Burkhart in his stimulating book, *The Freedom to Become Yourself*, says, "*You are you*. The *real you* is your link with God. You are the image of God, you are of God, you are the Divine life expressed in you, the person."

Emil Brunner rightly maintains that the mystery of self continues to baffle and bless us. There are two "I's" that compete for supremacy. The big "I," the Creator "I am" and the small "i." The temptation of the individual is to capitalize his own "i," thus becoming, at least for himself, the center of all reality and purpose. The observations and learning experiences on the college campus should enable one to differentiate between the capital "I" representing God and the small "i" representing self.

In discovering self, the student learns to curb his appetites, control his impulses and cultivate his emotions. He encounters a new discipline—the discipline of freedom. Good discipline is always more of a teacher than a policeman.

Even so, many are the attempts of students and people in general to escape themselves. The last person with whom many of us would care to shake hands is one's self.

There is a familiar story of a beggar who every day sat across the street from an artist's studio. Noticing the man asking for alms day after day, the able artist became interested and began studying the beggar's ritual. At last he was challenged to paint his impressions of the man. When the picture was finished he sent for the disheveled soul to come to his studio. Reluctantly, the haggard and hungry man obliged and as he stood gazing at the life-sized portrait asked, "Who is it?" Slowly as if comprehending the artist's interpretation, he ventured, "Is it me? Can it be me?" "Yes," replied the artist, "that's the man I see in you." Gratefully the neglected man replied, "If that's the man you see, that's the man I'll be!"

Among other places, the disciplined learning center we call college is in reality a hall of mirrors, a studio wherein dedicated and skillful teachers, glimpsing the potential of their students, challenge them in myriad ways to attain their capacities. As Alexander Pope, commenting on Aristotle's belief that a statue was imprisoned in every block of marble, said:

> Then take him to develop, if you can
> And hew the block off, and get out the man.

The challenge of a college education is to respect and respond to truth. The college, of course, is not the only harbinger of truth, but being a highly disciplined community, the campus is populated by diligent searchers for truth. Any conscientious student, irrespective of his field of study, has a passion for truth.

Truth is more than a clever definition about a place, being, or thing; it is the ultimate reality concerning that place, being, or thing. Truth is more than a carefully gleaned sheath of facts on a subject; it is the subject. Truth transcends opinion as sun the clouds. Truth is more than temporal knowledge; it is eternal wisdom.

Plato said that "Truth is a fair and durable thing."

"Truth," warned George Eliot, "has rough flavors if we bite it through."

" 'You will know the truth,' " said Jesus, " 'and the truth will make you free.' " (John 8:32.)

Elton Trueblood is correct in maintaining that "In no field is truth available except to those who have met the conditions."[3] How true of the gamut of life. Think of the silly devices we use, the rituals we practice, and the notions we conceive, in an attempt to postpone the inevitable encounter with truth. As children, truth is imposed upon us by adults, largely by our parents. This is a parental responsibility. However, as we grow older, we must discover truth for ourselves.

Unlike Pilate who confronted truth but once, daily truth stands before us. What is our choice? What is the truth about the Christian life? What is the truth about human relations? What is the truth about the church? Truth must be the impelling motive of action in all of our relationships if man is to live and serve with dignity and distinction.

The French critic, Vinet, once reported that people generally loved truth as Frederick the Great loved music. Actually, he was not fond of music at all, only the flute—*his* flute! It is tragic when we listen only to our own tunes of truth.

The challenge of a college education is the challenge to commit oneself to the ever-deepening concerns of life. Regardless of one's heritage or schooling, he is not educated until he learns how to live. And one of the most important lessons we all need to learn is that man cannot live by bread alone. The gadgets and gaieties of man can not ultimately satisfy—only the words and promises of God.

During the war years, I was privileged to introduce to a large audience, Muriel Lester, founder of Kingsley Hall, London. Among other memories of her address is that of the story of her nephew, George Aglwin Hogg, which may be found in

---

[3]*Philosophy of Religion,* New York: Harper & Brothers, 1957.

the opening pages of her continued autobiography, *It So Happened.*[4]

Mr. Hogg had just finished Oxford. He took his savings together with a small legacy and bought ocean passage around the world. He hitchhiked across our country. In Texas he was picked up by Mr. Lacey of the American Bible Society, and taken to San Francisco where they boarded ship with Miss Lester.

Muriel Lester and George Hogg arrived in Shanghai in February, 1938. The city was a sorry sight and was seething with trouble. Life was painful and death lurked in the streets. Young George was fascinated by the Orientals. He had not been in Shanghai more than five days when he said to his aunt, "I'm sorry but I shan't be able to go on to India with you. I can't leave China."

He never did.

George Hogg studied the language, the mores, and the problems of the Chinese. He identified himself with the people. At last he was made head of the Bailie schools. Eventually he wrote the book, *I See a New China.*

Because of college training and experiences with college-trained people, a great host of men and women have been able to see with increasing vision the abiding problems of mankind. Before the temptations of exploitation and personal advancement many have said, "I'm sorry, but I shan't be able to go on. I am needed here. . . ."

Thomas Carlyle looked at his people and exclaimed, "England is a population of 27,000,000 people, mainly fools." In this utterance, we glimpse the unmistakable Carlyle. David Livingstone, the missionary-explorer, looked at the filth and rot of Africa and commented: "An unhappy people to whom I must dedicate my life."

---

[4] See *It So Happened,* by Muriel Lester. Copyright 1947 by Harper & Brothers. Used by permission.

There was a great difference of insight in the two men.

To students preparing to leave for college and university, may you seek to implement more legibly in your own life, the declaration to Timothy: "Do your best to present yourself to God as one approved, a workman who has no need to be ashamed, rightly handling the word of truth." (2 Timothy 2: 15.)

The Guest Room

"Where is my guest room?"

—Mark 14:13

A CHERISHED MEMORY of our country home is that of the guest chamber. This bedroom was seldom used. It was for company. Once a seminary student, who preached in the community during the summer, stayed three months in our home and occupied the guest room.

There was a reverence for this room. It was in this chamber that my parents and I prayed together on the morning I left for seminary. Then, too, I remember that practically every time I returned home, after committing myself to the ministry, instead of occupying my usual bedroom, Mother would suggest that I take the guest room. That old spare room is hallowed with memories.

This is more than sentimental reminiscing. There is a thread of genuine hospitality running through the record of our faith, frequently emanating from the hearthstones of devoted friends.

There are many such homes in our Bible. They give us pause in this day of efficiency apartments and compact houses when one can scarcely afford housing for his family, let alone the luxury of a guest room. However, despite our architectural advances and conveniences, the omission of the guest room in the modern home may yet result in spiritual penalties.

In the First Book of Kings, we find a remarkable reference to a guest room. Elijah had called the hand of King Ahab and furthermore he had prophesied a drought. Consequently, the prophet feared for his life and went into hiding. He became exceedingly hungry in his wanderings. At last he entered the village of Zarephath. There the prophet met a widow gathering sticks. Elijah called to her, " 'Bring me a morsel of bread. . . .'

" 'I have nothing baked, only a handful of meal in a jar, and a little oil in a cruse; . . . I am gathering a couple of sticks, that I may go in and prepare it for myself and my son, that we may eat it, and die.'

" 'Go and do as you have said; but first make me a little cake of it and bring it to me. . . . "The jar of meal shall not be spent, and the cruse of oil shall not fail. . . ." ' " (1 Kings 17: 11-14.)

The woman obeyed. The meal was multiplied. The oil was increased. They ate together for many days.

Subsequently the son of the widow was stricken unto death. The woman reasoned that she was being punished for previous sins, but Elijah said, " 'Give me your son.' " (1 Kings 17: 19.)

"And he took him from her bosom, and carried him up into the upper chamber, where he lodged, and laid him upon his own bed." (1 Kings 17:19.)

A miracle transpired. The body was restored to life and the widow exclaimed, " 'Now I know that you are a man of God, and that the word of the Lord in your mouth is truth.' " (1 Kings 17:24.)

" 'Come over to Macedonia and help us.' " (Acts 16:9.) Paul heard this voice while in Troas. He was both troubled and challenged. Troubled because no one had previously penetrated this part of the world with the gospel of Christ; challenged at the thought of preaching in a new world. He obeyed.

Paul and his company sailed to Philippi, a city of Macedonia and prominent among the Roman colonies. The first congregation that the Apostle found was one of women worshiping near a river. It was an attentive though not an impressive audience. He preached; they listened; they were converted. The women were baptized.

Among that little company was a lady by the name of Lydia, a prominent businesswoman, a "dealer in purple." She was probably engaged in the profitable business of merchandising expensive cloth. Thus we have a right to assume that she was a leading citizen in the community.

Now immediately upon her conversion, she said to Paul and his associates, " 'If you have judged me to be faithful to the Lord, come to my house and stay.' " (Acts 16:15.) They went. This marked the beginning of the church at Philippi. Paul always maintained a peculiar pride in this church.

Lydia had a church in her home.

" 'Go into the city, and a man carrying a jar of water will meet you; follow him, and wherever he enters, say to the householder, "The Teacher says, Where is my guest room, where I am to eat the passover with my disciples?" ' " (Mark 14:13-14.) This introduces one of the most intriguing scenes in the Scriptures. Jesus was preparing his disciples for a most meaningful farewell. Two of them were commissioned to go into Jerusalem and make ready for the passover.

Every Christian could wish he knew where the Master held the Last Supper. We read it was in a large upper room—but whose? I like to think that our Lord had a very dependable friend in Jerusalem—perhaps a shopkeeper—with whom he visited when in the Holy City. Doubtless this convert knew of coming events. I think, too, it is highly possible that this anonymous friend sent two of his servants to a given gate to watch for and to escort the disciples to his house. Whatever the circumstances, the fact remains that Jesus chose the guest room of some wonderful home to establish the family meal of the church. It is perfectly logical to assume that after the resurrection of Jesus, his disciples and other converts reassembled in this same room, waiting for his return.

It is highly significant that Christians everywhere should assemble today, World Communion Sunday, to share the spirit of love dramatized in that ancient upper room. In that little room the maps of the world were changed and the aspirations of men challenged. Jesus girded himself with a towel and bathed the feet of his followers. Hence the towel, a symbol of service, is dropped at the foot of the cross—a symbol of sacrifice.

Communion between man and his Maker is at the very center of every known religion. Moslems have their prayer mats; Hindus, their prayer wheels. Jews keep the Passover; Catholics place great emphasis upon the Mass. Quakers do not use the consecrated elements of bread and wine as do many others, but they observe the fellowship of silence.

Communion has held a strategic place in the history of Disciples. It was about the communion table that the vision of our people appeared and from which our concept of ecumenicity emanated. From the day of Thomas Campbell's open invitation for all Christians to share in the Lord's Supper until this good hour, Disciples, in the vast majority of instances, have practiced open communion, realizing that, irrespective of one's conviction or church affiliation, here, in the mystery of

the fellowship, Christ comes even as of old to bless and to
bind hearts together with and in love.

What happens at communion is a question that has perenni-
ally plagued the Christian. In the Middle Ages an interpretation known as transubstantiation developed. It is still the
official doctrine of the Roman Catholic church. It teaches that
when the priest holds the bread and wine, these elements are
miraculously and literally transformed into the substances of
the body of Christ. Thus the living Christ enters the worshiper as he partakes of the physical emblems.

Martin Luther, who could not accept this interpretation,
devised the term "consubstantiation." It teaches that whereas
Christ's body is not the bread, Christ is nonetheless spiritually
present in the bread. To explain this, he used the illustration
of a red-hot iron. The heat is not the iron but it is in it. Even
so, Christ touches the faithful hearts of those who share in the
meal.

Zwingli looked upon communion as the visible emblems of
an invisible reality. John Calvin spoke of the sacraments as
"seals," a term which is best understood in the light of commercial transactions.

Disciples have accepted the ordinance of Christian communion as the center of their fellowship. It is a symbol that
speaks of Christ's love and presence. It is a portrayal of sacrificial love which every Christian is committed to imitate. In
Appointment with God, J. B. Phillips says,

Although we have in Holy Communion far more than a tradition,
because we have in it something which is alive in itself, yet it has of
course a value simply as a tradition, that is, as something men consider
worth passing on from generation to generation. But it is unique in that
the other end of it is, so to speak, *alive,* intimately joined to the very life
of the Son of God Himself.[1]

[1]From *Appointment With God,* J. B. Phillips. Copyright 1954 by The Mac-
millan Company. Used by permission.

Jesus is present in spirit at the appointed time and hence the Lord's table is spread every Sunday. The words of institution become very personal: "Let a man examine himself, and so eat of the bread and drink of the cup." (1 Corinthians 11:28.) Thus to most Protestants, it becomes a great confessional.

There is a contagion about Christian communion that transcends geography and personal faith. A few months ago a visitor worshiped with us and, during the fellowship period that followed, presented himself and asked if I remembered him. It was with regret that I acknowledged I did not. Then he said, "You served me communion in Jerusalem." In a real sense everyone is served communion in Jerusalem.

On this World-Wide Communion Sunday, Christ would make of our hearts an upper room. Marie Elmore Baxter has expressed it in her prayer:

> O Holy Christ, come now and bless
> This feast here spread, we pray;
> Touch with Thy tender loving hands
> Our hearts of common clay;
> Reveal Thy presence to us now,
> Unveil Thy mystery,
> That we may know celestial joy
> In full sufficiency.
>
> Here at Thy table we have met,
> Confessing our deep need
> To share this testamental board,
> Regardless of our creed;
> Make in our hearts an Upper Room
> Where we Thy face may see;
> Come now, O Holy Christ, to bless
> As we remember Thee.[2]

[2]"A Communion Prayer," from *The Christian-Evangelist*, September 29, 1954. Used by permission.

The Challenge of the Ministry

And how are they to hear without a preacher? And how can men preach unless they be sent?

—Romans 10:14-15

THERE IS a dramatic story concerning the life and influence of King George V. In the latter years of his reign it was his custom to broadcast a Christmas message to the Empire. During one of these broadcasts, when the ears of the world were waiting to hear the voice of the king, an engineer observed that an important wire had snapped. America was cut off. Time was of the essence. Suddenly, as though nudged by an angel, a mechanic seized the broken wires. Holding one in each hand, he was thus able to complete the circuit which permitted the royal message to be transmitted to America. The voice of the king passed through the body of the engineer.

In the broken connections of our world how can the Word of the Lord be heard unless it passes through the preacher? In a less dramatic, though equally indispensable position, ministers of God have stood through the centuries. With one hand extended upward to the heavenly Father and the other reaching down to human need, they have frequently been able to keep open the circuit of communication.

The Protestant church has been confused in its concept of the ministry. Schools have not known whether they were preparing competitive salesmen, or statesmen for the Universal Church. Society has been perplexed. Are ministers untouchables, or have they been overly touched?

H. Richard Niebuhr reminds us in *The Purpose of the Church and Its Ministry* that whereas some ninety medical schools are apparently adequate to supply the United States and Canada with physicians and surgeons, there are twice as many theological schools, not to mention Bible colleges and institutes. Yet there is an unprecedented shortage of ministers. According to Elmer G. Million, Protestant churches of America will need to recruit and train 618,750 new ministers by 1975.[1] It is estimated that there are some 15,000 vacant parishes and pulpits in America.[2]

This condition did not come about overnight, nor will it be corrected by spontaneous convention resolutions. Shifts in population, the status of the American home, automation, emphasis on financial security, scouting of schools by business and industry for the more brilliant students, together with the misconceptions and disadvantages of the ministry, have all contributed to our deficit and dilemma. Not the least of the offenders is the church itself. Congregations have failed to challenge, recruit and train their finest young people for the Christian ministry.

Professor Wesley Schrader of Yale Divinity School shocked America when he published in the August 20, 1956, issue of *Life Magazine* the amazing and much discussed article "Why Ministers Are Breaking Down." His main thesis was: too many ministers have too many roles to play.

[1] See *National Council Outlook*, May, 1957.
[2] From *The College of the Bible Quarterly*, Lexington, Kentucky, Vol. XXXIV, January, 1957.

Writing from a somewhat different point of view, James B. Moore in *Harper's Magazine* maintains: "The unhappiness of many a clergyman is, I think, not due so much to overwork, or too many demands, as it is to conflicts between what he is expected to be and do and say, and what he would rather be and do and say."[3]

Likewise, there has been confusion concerning what constitutes a call to the Christian ministry. There are instances, of course, where individuals experienced a peculiar confirmation of their desire to enter the ministry. Perhaps a revealing tragedy, a transforming miracle, or an emotional ecstasy gave clarity to the call. However, this can also be said of those who enter any honorable vocation. "Every Christian," says Henry Sloane Coffin, "is called by the Master to follow him, and that following may be in a carpenter's shop, as well as in preaching and teaching."[4] Sincere disciples, regardless of talent or skill, wealth or wisdom, should respond to the obvious will of God as did Isaiah, " 'Here I am! Send me.' " (Isaiah 6:8.)

In a real sense, however, there is a uniqueness about the call to the Christian ministry in that it was deemed essential by God and ordained by Christ and the primitive church. The man who thinks himself into the ministry, carefully prepares, and is willing to submit to rigorous discipline, receives incalculable compensations. He thrills at the privilege of proclaiming the story of God's grace through Christ. He rejoices at the thought that he has been duly set apart to minister to the needs of people in the name of the Saving Person. And so, with fear and trembling, the minister takes his place in that

---

[3]From "Why Young Ministers Are Leaving the Church," by James B. Moore in *Harper's Magazine*, July, 1957. Used by permission.

[4]Henry Sloane Coffin, "His Call," from *The Ministry*, J. Richard Spann, Editor. New York and Nashville: Abingdon Press, 1949.

noble line of men and women through the wondrous ages who have felt that the spirit of God was upon them.

Moreover, not unlike other vocations and professions, the ministry is laden with disadvantages. To begin with, one cannot regulate his life. It is regulated for him. The minister is one of the most vulnerable men in the community. No profession is more exposed to the whims of society. Much of the minister's time is spent with neurotics or replying to the criticisms of the uninformed. Committee meetings demand his attention. He can do very little about his economic welfare, except to move. He is often a lonely man, for he is the only member of his congregation who does not have a minister.

He is by nature, tradition, and training a crusader, starting many things for which he is never credited and exposed to many which are incompatible with his philosophy of life. He lives so intimately with his work that his disappointments and heartaches frequently prejudice his family against the church.

Despite the misconceptions and heavy demands associated with this high calling, there is, nevertheless, an irresistibility about the Christian ministry. Many men, however unworthy, cannot resist the challenge of becoming spokesmen for God; to disassociate themselves from the connivings of the world; to be free to propagate the spirit of Christ.

The 1958 *Year Book of American Churches* reports 293,550 ordained Protestant clergymen in the continental United States.

As Dr. Douglas Horton said: "In general, a community is not better than its churches. In general, a church is not better than its minister. In general, a minister is not better than his training."[5]

---

[5]Douglas Horton, "Today's Education of Tomorrow's Ministers" (an address delivered at The College of The Bible, Lexington, Kentucky, October 31, 1956). *The College of the Bible Quarterly*, Vol. XXXIV, January, 1957.

Against this background then, let us concern ourselves with the challenge of the Christian ministry.

Ours is the challenge to perpetuate the ministry of revelation. Lord Tennyson was not the last to exclaim, "I count above all things else a fresh vision of God." Like Philip we cry, " 'Lord, show us the Father, and we shall be satisfied.' " (John 14:8.)

People of our day thirst and hunger for a fresh presentation of God; not a declaration about the heavenly Father, but for an affirmation of the Father's nature and the assurance of his nearness and mercy. Every phase of the ministry is a challenge to present the genuineness of God. A discerning minister humbly assumes his responsibilities knowing that he stands in an awesome line of loyal souls whose primary purpose was to reveal the Father.

Horace Bushnell was a courageous and contagious servant of God. A friend once remarked, "Dr. Bushnell, I think when the angel nearest the throne sees you coming he will say to the Master, 'There comes a man you know.' " Modestly, though quickly, the venerable gentleman replied, "I trust so, and I am sure I shall know him!" He who speaks for God must know God if he is to share the supreme revelation.

Ours is likewise the challenge to share in the ministry of redemption. Wendell Phillips, son of a distinguished Harvard graduate, was known as a "reformer and agitator." He was persistent in his search for truth and justice. It was said that after the erudite orator gave a moving address, a newspaperman approached him saying, "Mr. Phillips, I wish to publish this address and will do so if you will leave off the last paragraph"—to which the conscientious man in his irritation shouted, "Leave off the last paragraph? I wrote the whole speech just to say that."[6]

---

[6]From *Good Ministers of Jesus,* by William Fraser McDowell. Copyright 1917 by Abingdon Press. Used by permission.

Grand and glorious as are the personalities that people the Book, they are not to be compared with the Man who completes the Book. Paul sensed this when he said, "I decided to know nothing among you except Jesus Christ and him crucified." (1 Corinthians 2:2.)

John Bunyan, after lying in prison twelve years for preaching the truth as he saw it, was told by the jailer, "John, you can go free if you will agree to quit preaching." Bunyan answered, "I am determined, Almighty God being my help and shield, yet to suffer, if frail life might continue so long, even till moss shall grow over my eyebrows, rather than to violate my faith and make a continual butchery of my conscience!"[7]

This prophetic and personal sense of responsibility has characterized the more courageous fathers and reformers, prophets and priests of the church in every generation and community. Those who have determined, and are determining, the quality of our Christian faith have known that the all-inclusive query concerning their ministry must forever be, What kind of Jesus do I preach?

Ours is also the challenge to share in the ministry of reconciliation. One never ceases to wonder at the completeness of the Word in the Bible. This Word, as John Keats says of the poetic word, rings like a bell giving tongue to time and voice to eternity. Reconciliation is a comforting chalice from which we unworthily and sometimes unwillingly drink. The secrets of religion, the depths of faith, and the breadth of love, all find expression in this revealing Word.

The late Joseph Fort Newton declared there were but three avenues open to the individual and "the joy of life" is dependent upon the choice. They are: rebellion, resignation, and reconciliation.

[7]From *To Fulfill This Ministry* by William C. Martin. Copyright 1948 by Abingdon Press. Used by permission.

Many are the common demonstrations of rebellion. We are familiar with them. They range from temper tantrums of children to international icebergs. Life is likewise strewn with those who have resigned, and stand with their backs to life. Only the growing Christian can testify to the twin miracles of love and forgiveness which not only produce harmony and good will but restore peace of mind and strength of soul.

A couple sought my counsel. Like many other marriages, theirs had become a burden rather than a joy. Having long since learned that an effective counselor is one who listens more than he talks, I was amazed at the completeness of their criticisms. Now and again, I inserted a suggestion. Our conference concluded with a season of prayer, each praying in turn. When the couple left the church, I noticed they walked to their automobile hand in hand. The man opened the door for his wife. Later she told me that she was not only surprised but shocked to have him open the car door. This was the beginning of reconciliation.

But deeper than harmony between humans is harmony between the individual and his God. Paul wrote, "We beseech you on behalf of Christ, be reconciled to God." (2 Corinthians 5:20.) Regardless of the cruelties and casualties of life, God is forever willing and eager to forgive and to reclaim. Are we reconciled to God? Do we really believe in him and trust him? There are hours of satisfying insight and ecstasy which move us to mountain peaks of transfiguration only later to settle down to the same old routine and to become transfixed by our own whims and wills. The minister is constantly striving to bring encouragement to his people, inviting them—indeed, urging them—to be reconciled to God.

Not only are ministers challenged to persuade their people to become reconciled to God, but they, themselves, must become reconciled to their own situations. They, too, are chal-

lenged to remember the incarnation. William Ellery Channing
was one of the most brilliant preachers of the nineteenth
century. Emerson was charmed by his eloquence. He was
sometimes referred to as ". . . the star of the American
church." Yet throughout his long and distinguished ministry
at the Federal Street Church in Boston (1803-1842), he was
plagued by ill-health, which forced him to take frequent and
long vacations. Nevertheless, during a period of unusual illness he was able to say: "A hoarseness has closed my mouth
for two Sundays, and I know not when liberty of speech will
be given me. Happily, the spirit is free, and I try to turn my
solitude to some account."[8]

Interestingly enough, William Henry Channing, a nephew
of William Ellery, in many ways a kindred spirit who was
greatly influenced by his uncle, set forth his philosophy of life
in this trenchant statement:

> To live content with small means; to seek elegance rather than luxury,
> and refinement rather than fashion; to be worthy, not respectable, and
> wealthy, not rich; to listen to stars and birds, babes and sages with open
> heart; to study hard; to think quietly, act frankly, talk gently, await
> occasions, hurry never; in a word, to let the spiritual, unbidden and
> unconscious, grow up through the common—this is my symphony.[9]

This is but a golden glimpse of the Galilean who said,
" 'Not as I will, but as thou wilt.' " (Matthew 26:39.)

Moreover ours is the challenge to share in the ministry of
rescue. Doubtless, the minister's supreme task is here expressed, " 'For the Son of man came to seek and to save the
lost.' " (Luke 19:10.) Jesus was on a rescue mission. He was
constantly seeking to save men from their folly and sin by introducing them to God and his way of life. The minister of

---

[8]From *Memoir* of William Ellery Channing, Vol. II. Boston: Wm. Crosby and
H. P. Nichols.   London: John Chapman, 1848.

[9]Newell Dwight Hillis, *Right Living as a Fine Art*.   New York, Chicago and
Toronto: Fleming H. Revell Company, 1903.

Jesus Christ is commissioned to seek out the lost of his community, and they are not all on Skid Row. They may be found in every neighborhood and walk of life—and in every church.

There is something wonderful and reassuring about a rescue story. The eyes of the world rest on any disaster and applaud the heroes who emerge. No triumph of land, sea, or air, however, corresponds to what transpired at Calvary. Truth and falsehood, sin and saviorhood, were locked in a deadly duel outside Jerusalem. The destiny of man was in the balance and God came to the rescue. As Georgia Harkness says, "The cross means the meeting point of suffering with love, and God's way of conquering evil through suffering love."[10] The miracle of the cross is the miracle of God's redeeming love. Every minister must not only face the cross himself but also challenge his people to come and stand by his side in the light of the cross.

A journalist was writing a series of articles on Oxford University. During the course of their appearance a correspondent wrote in to ask, "Please tell us what Oxford is to the man who is in earnest; say to General Booth, or any other man like him in earnestness of his life?" In effect the correspondent is asking, This is all very well for a university graduate but what of us who live on Ninth Street?

To everyone who is in earnest, regardless of station or stature, the cross says you have a Savior. "And he died for all, that those who live might live no longer for themselves but for him who for their sake died and was raised." (2 Corinthians 5:15.)

The challenge of the Christian ministry is to tell "the old, old story of Jesus and his love."

In his vigorous book, *Adventurous Preaching,* James H. Robinson relates an experience with Harry Emerson Fosdick.

[10]From *Understanding the Christian Faith.* Abingdon Press, 1957.

The eminent pulpiteer had retired from Riverside Church, New York, but not from personal responsibilities. Dr. Robinson was interested in raising money for a Harlem Community Center and asked Dr. Fosdick to help him. The only place available for a preliminary meeting was a night club. Before their meeting was over, some of the "clubbers" dropped in and waited for the churchmen to drop out. Robinson says that the presence of the mighty preacher illuminated the dingy, dimly lighted room. His talk made a wonderful impression on one of the waiters who was not a churchgoer but who volunteered his night's wages to the project. "He makes everything so clear," said the humble man. "I wish I had heard him years ago. That man has persuaded me. I've got to have a part in this work. Somehow, I want to be a better man. . . ."[11]

To confront every person with the claims of Christ on his life is the challenge of the ministry.

God's Minutemen

" 'Rise and go. . .' "
—*Acts 8:26*

P A U L R E V E R E, Boston silversmith and engraver, lives in history because of his courageous role in the American Revolution. He was an active leader in the Boston Tea Party. The patriot was also one of thirty "north-end mechanics" who patrolled the streets at night to observe British troop movements. He is more clearly remembered for his famous midnight ride from Charlestown to Lexington, Massachusetts, April 18-19, 1775.

However, Revere's ride would have been but a foolish loss of sleep had it not been for the co-operation and courage of the minutemen of Massachusetts. These anonymous heroes, though volunteers, and without formal military training, were nevertheless committed to fight at "a minute's notice." Their blows were especially felt in the battle of Lexington. The revolution begun by the minutemen is incomplete. In the continuing revolution let us not forget the strength of spontaneity and the contagion of courage.

Humanly speaking, the welfare of the blessed community has always depended upon the willingness of its converts to

witness. Early Christians gave themselves in dangerous earnestness to the propagation of the message of Christ. The
early church was a witnessing fellowship. These knights of
the burning heart knew in whom they believed, and joyously
shared their faith.

Our text contains the divine command to Philip, one of
God's enviable minutemen. He was a deacon in the Jerusalem
church. Philip was directed to leave the Holy City and travel
southward toward Gaza. As he journeyed, he observed an ap-
proaching chariot, the principal occupant being none other
than secretary of the treasury of a North African state called
Ethiopia. The pilgrim was returning from worship in Jerusalem. This, together with the fact that he was reading from
the Prophet Isaiah, suggests that he could have been a Jewish
proselyte. Whereas we cannot be certain of his religious
status, this we know: Philip encountered a man who was dili-
gently seeking a way of life. Recognizing his opportunity,
God's ambassador asked, " 'Do you understand what you are
reading?' " The stranger answered, " 'How can I, unless some
one guides me?' " (Acts 8:31.)

The eunuch invited Philip to join him in the carriage. Apparently this royal official had been perplexed by Isaiah's
words and he said to Philip, " 'About whom, pray, does the
prophet say this, about himself or about some one else?' Then
Philip opened his mouth, and beginning with this scripture
he told him the good news of Jesus." (Acts 8:34-35.)

The conversion and baptism of the celebrity by Philip is a
vivid reminder of the importance of personal obedience to
divine direction. Out of this experience came the Coptic
church which was, and is to this day, the oldest branch of the
church.

This incident also suggests God's method of building up the
Christian community. There are but two effective ways to

promote and support worthy enterprises. One is to live it. The other is to talk it. No amount of advertising by the church will bring people to Christ unless members of the congregation sense and accept personal responsibility for people.

We of this technical age are inclined to frown on a method as old and slow as personal encounter. Yet we all know there is no substitute for the communal approach. It has been called evangelism by geometrical progression. Should one need to be convinced of the soundness of the system let him take pencil and paper and start with twelve, the number of Christ's disciples, and compute the result if the number were doubled each year. He will soon discover that within a generation— thirty years or so—the total population of the world could be reached for Christ. In fact, some of us committed ourselves to a program years ago: The World for Christ in One Generation. Mathematically, it is possible. The difficulty, of course, is that men are not as dependable as digits and the human equation breaks down.

Another layman whose mighty ministry condemns us is Andrew. He, too, was a humble man, yet this soft-spoken disciple said to his impetuous brother, Peter, " 'We have found the Messiah.' " (John 1:41.) In contrast, we volunteer information and misinformation on everything from sports to sputnik and yet are reluctant to commend Jesus Christ to our relatives and friends.

Let us remember also that it was Andrew who, while thoughtfully moving among the multitude, discovered a bashful boy with a lunch—"five barley loaves and two fish" (John 6:9)—and brought him to Jesus. This concerned disciple helped to set in motion the miracle of feeding the 5,000. Later, this same dedicated follower intercepted and introduced the Greeks who came asking for a conference with Jesus.

Still another type of layman needed today is described by Paul during his ministry in Corinth: "Crispus, the ruler of the synagogue, believed in the Lord, together with all his household." (Acts 18:8.) Whereas Philip was a roving evangelist and Andrew a quiet, effective home missionary, here we find an official of the church becoming concerned. Officers of the church are frequently the last to commit themselves to frontline responsibilities. If elders, deacons, deaconesses, leaders of the church are not converted to the ways of Christ, then the church becomes just another club with minimum dues, minimum expectations, and maximum demands.

As always, the church is dependent upon laymen to accomplish its mission. Christianity is pre-eminently a layman's religion. Jesus took a cross section of men and transformed them into the cross-bearers of the ages. The cross respects no protocol.

The Archbishop of Canterbury, Geoffrey Francis Fisher, addressing the second assembly of the World Council of Churches at Evanston, said, "There are only two groups of people in the modern world who know what they are after. One, quite frankly, is the Communist and the other, equally frankly, is the convinced Christian. The rest of the world are amiable nonentities."

The world situation demands new men—churchmen who are interested in introducing men to the Master rather than occupying the moon. Christ calls men who are more concerned about spiritual osmosis than guided missiles. The ultimate balance of power lies not in Moscow, nor in London, nor in Washington, but in Almighty God.

Four decades ago, all the known Communists in the world could have assembled in your living room. For the most part, they were suspects and were wanted by the police. They controlled not a single government, agency, or territory. Today, there are literally millions of card-carrying Communists, and they control one-third of the world's people. This has happened in less than fifty years, and we have permitted it to happen by not moving into the vacuums of the world with the positive redeeming message of Jesus Christ.

Moreover, we are witnessing "population explosions." Statisticians indicate there were only 200,000,000 people on the earth at the time of our Lord's birth. The twentieth century opened with a population approximated at 1,600,000,000. In the last fifty years the net growth of population has been over 800,000,000. Furthermore, by 1975 we must assimilate an additional 60,000,000 Americans. The birth rate of our country in the years to come will approximate that of India. While rural population will decrease, urban population will increase. Such realistic facts should shock the church out of its complacency and fill its members with genuine Christian concern. What is the import of all this for our day? What do the minutemen of yesterday say to the modern man? Philip obeyed, yes! Andrew introduced relatives and friends to the Master, and Crispus became more concerned. But what about ourselves?

To begin with, these and other stalwart men exemplified a commitment to Christ that was all-consuming and contagious. Nothing less than total commitment will be adequate today. All too often, as churchmen, we demonstrate a partial commitment. Frequently it is one of convenience and minimum cost. But the church of the Lord Jesus Christ cannot redeem the world with part-time Christians. We can spend ourselves in such worthy undertakings as the United Fund, local councils for health, March of Dimes, and community duties, and still fail miserably to meet the commands of a Christian. Christian minutemen are committed to the church.

D. T. Niles reminds us of the heartbroken father, Mathew Sands, praying on his knees. In his hands he held a telegram which read: "Your son David reported missing believed dead." Mathew Sands was inarticulate as he quietly recalled the life of his son, a pilot in the Air Force. At last he turned the telegram over and wrote on the back of it, "All that I have and all that I am, I give to God and for his service."

These words of recommitment brought comfort to his harrowed heart. Presently the telephone rang. It conveyed the interest of a neighboring university in Mathew Sands, a retired priest. En route to the university for an interview, Mathew Sands came upon an abandoned church. Beside it a sign read, "For sale by auction." He entered the church to pray and while there decided to buy it and restore it to its high and holy purposes.

Later another man entered, Andrew Jelks. He, too, had come to appraise the property. If acquired, he planned to turn the building into "Andy's Amusement Arcade." Anyway, Sands determined to write the trustees and make them an offer.

When the day of the sale arrived, a curious and concerned group of people gathered about the church. Mathew Sands, standing among them, put his hand into his pocket only to find the letter addressed to the trustees. In his confused state of mind, he had inadvertently enclosed the wire from the War Office instead of his offer. He was disappointed and disgusted with himself, but it was too late. While quietly reminiscing, the man in charge of the sale finally announced that the church had been sold to Mathew Sands, declaring that his was the highest offer. Then the spokesman for the occasion made bold to read aloud the bid: "All that I have and all that I am, I give to God and for his service."[1]

---

[1]From *The Gospel of the Resurrection* by D. T. Niles. Published, 1954, The Westminster Press. Used by permission.

Is not this the meaning of commitment—dying to self? Christians are called to give themselves and their substance to God for the fulfillment of his purposes through the church. Commitment is never complete until it finds completion in the individual.

Committed men stand ready to answer the myriad calls of Christ. Like Philip, they rise and go. While at Crystal Lake, Michigan, the summer of 1956, we encountered a number of interesting Christians, among them Mr. and Mrs. Joe Bashore from the Far West. He answered his country's call in World War II, and was wounded in action. Upon release from service, he returned to his ranch, assuming his usual responsibilities. In addition he learned more about engineering and construction. When the United Christian Missionary Society (Disciples of Christ) needed builders to go to the Belgian Congo, he volunteered. He qualified. Consequently Joe Bashore, his wife, and their three small children went to Africa.

During the 1957 Cleveland International Convention of the Christian Churches (Disciples of Christ), Dr. Fiers, president of their missionary society, received a cablegram stating that Joe Bashore had lost his right hand in an accident.

He did not have to go to Africa. He had a good farm and an attractive family, but he felt in his heart he had to go. Even as he learned that the service of his country was costly, so now his church. When I heard of the unfortunate happening, I recalled Paul's magnificent sentence to the Galatians: "Henceforth let no man trouble me; for I bear on my body the marks of Jesus." (Galatians 6:17.)

Another evidence of commitment is acceptance of responsibility. Laymen must increasingly sense and demonstrate Christian responsibility. Christians have always been responsible for mankind. When we lose a sense of responsibility we lose reverence for worship and for life. As churchmen not only are we responsible for mankind but we are also responsible to Jesus Christ.

Le Feu by Henri Barbusse, English translation, *Under Fire*, by Fitzwater Wray, is a strange novel of World War I. Dramatically, the French author describes the condition of the men as they listened to the "rattle of death." No Man's Land was a sorry sight. In the chapter entitled "The Refuge," Barbusse records this conversation:

"Listen, Dominque. You've led a bad life. You cribbed things, and you were quarrelsome when drunk. You've dirtied *your* ticket in the police register, properly.

"As for me, I've no more family than you have. I've nobody, except Louise—and she isn't a relative of mine, seeing we're not married. And there are no convictions against me, beyond a few little military jobs. There's nothing on my name."

"Well, what about it? *I* don't care. . ."

"I'm going to tell you. Take my name. Take it—I give it you; as long as neither of us has any family."

"Your name?"

"Yes. . ."

"Oh, Christ!" said the other, "you'd do that? You'd—that—well, old chap, that beats all!"[2]

This unglossed story of common concern and love reminds us of the One who took our sins and our poor records and buried them forever; and who has through grace given us the name "Christian." Real Christians are those who remember this transfer of name and transformation in life and are grateful. Their gratitude is manifested in their obligation to spread the good news.

---

[2]From *Under Fire*, by Henri Barbusse. Copyright 1917 by E. P. Dutton & Company, Inc. Used by permission.

Prerogatives of Protestantism

And we all, with unveiled face, beholding the glory
of the Lord, are being changed into his likeness from
one degree of glory to another; for this comes from
the Lord who is the Spirit.

—2 Corinthians 3:18

ABOUT NOON on October 31, 1517, a stocky Augustinian monk nailed his ninety-five theses on the north door of the Castle Church in Wittenberg, Germany. An ordinary act, for the door also served as a bulletin board. To all practical observers, it was just a routine matter.

It was an unusual statement, however. It was a challenge to debate certain propositions ranging, as Roland Bainton says, from "complaints" to "the cries of a wrestler in the night." Though the church itself may not have recognized the implications, it was primarily the declaration of a man's faith. Even Pope Leo X, when he heard about it, quipped, "Luther is a drunken German. He will feel different when he is sober."[1] However, the printer, recognizing that this was no ordinary document, ran off extra copies and circulated them throughout Germany. Thus, what was originally intended as a priest's protest revived previous criticisms of the church, ignited others, and ultimately resulted in the religious revolution that produced Protestantism.

---

[1] See *Here I Stand* by Roland Bainton. Abingdon Press, 1950, p. 85.

Protestantism stems from at least two sources: one is from those churches that had their beginnings in the mighty Reformation of the sixteenth and seventeenth centuries; the other is from the original Church of the apostles which has continued for nearly 2,000 years (the precious remnant, a genuine and growing revival of life and faith) and connects us with the apostolic fellowship. This latter is what Protestants mean when they say, "I believe in the holy catholic church."

As we observe the festival of Reformation, not in the negatives of separation, nor as a conceited and complete accomplishment, but as an expression of free followers of Christ, it should be encouraging to review some of the prerogatives of Protestantism.

A unique prerogative of a Protestant is the privilege of being his own priest. When Luther said, "Here I stand, I cannot do otherwise," he uttered and demonstrated a peculiar right, that of a man, irrespective of his station or stature, having free access to the throne of God. Christ alone was and is the high priest. In a day when independent religious thought and action were punishable by death, this heroic and courageous monk took his stand for personal commitment to Jesus Christ, the sole head of the Church.

We need to remember that it was not always popular to state one's faith. Now, with more than 281,687 congregations scattered across America, it does not require spectacular courage to profess Protestantism. But in the sixteenth century, it was heresy for a man to say he was his own priest. It was more than a stubborn stand; it was a positive stand for that which ennobles man.

Moreover, may we never forget that as seeking, free souls, unencumbered by superstition, magic, indulgences, hazards, and costliness of purgatory, penitent followers can call on the name of the Lord Jesus Christ, and, believing, be saved.

Another prerogative of the Protestant is his freedom to pursue truth as symbolized by the open Bible. Again it is difficult for us to realize that there was a time when the Bible was "inside information," capable of being studied and interpreted only by priests. Two hundred years before Luther, John Wycliffe took an early lead in the translation of the Vulgate Bible into English. When he fell into disfavor, evangels went into the streets, preaching from texts translated by Wycliffe. Later critics dug up and burned his bones.

To the Reformers the Bible was not only the norm of their Christian beliefs but also a guide to their daily living.

Both Roman Catholicism and Protestantism are founded on the New Testament. There is, however, a significant difference, namely, Catholicism claims the right to develop and interpret the sources of its faith, which is tantamount to placing the church above the authority of the Scriptures. Protestantism is more flexible, although through necessity the church also becomes an interpreter of the Scriptures. Protestants have not only given the world an open Bible, but they also read it in freedom.

Henry Ward Beecher's mother died when he was a small boy. One day, during a difficult period in his development, he was rummaging through an old trunk in his father's study where he found a bundle of letters written by his mother to his father: a record of their courtship and love. They were beautiful letters and through them Beecher became better acquainted with his mother and he loved her all the more.

Similarly, Protestants are free to exercise the privilege of examining the love letters of the centuries, the Bible: the story of man's search for God and God's love for man. Thus he is enabled to become better acquainted with the Father and with himself.

Closely allied with the pursuit of freedom and inquiry is, of course, the matter of spiritual growth. Protestantism is not a finished revival. It is a continuous process of reforming man and challenging him to express himself about Jesus Christ.

Roman Catholics reserve the right to interpret truth; Protestants challenge their members to discover truth. For instance, consider the dogma of the Virgin Mary's assumption as proclaimed by Pope Pius XII. According to this modern pronouncement, all Roman Catholics must accept the belief that Mary's physical body ascended to heaven. Disbelief is considered heresy. Any intelligent person, seeking truth and satisfaction, is compelled to ask, "Why did it require two thousand years to make such a startling discovery?" For the Protestant, truth can never be superimposed; it must be sought and experienced.

Luther was impelled to share his Lord. The Reformers were flaming evangels. They broke through the rigid systems of theology. The Reformation reiterated the authority of the good news and the responsibility of the individual for its communication. Paul's declaration has been a constant reminder that Christ "died for all, that those who live might live no longer for themselves, but for him who for their sake died and was raised." (2 Corinthians 5:15.) Here is justification by faith. Here we see that faith is the victory. The thief dying on the cross said, "'Jesus, remember me. . . .'" (Luke 23:2.) Faith was all that he had. He had no credentials, save those of crime. But our Lord heard his penitent cry and replied, "'Truly, I say to you, today you will be with me in Paradise.'" (Luke 23:43.)

Luther was not a thief. He was a devoted parish priest and professor of divinity in the University of Wittenberg, but he felt himself unworthy of God's redeeming grace and love. The Apostle Paul also was tortured by his sense of unworthiness. He declared himself to be chief among sinners. "God, be merciful to me a sinner!" (Luke 18:13) was the petition of the publican. And did not Jesus say that this man was justified rather than the Pharisee who proudly recited his autobiography?

"Remember me," is not only the spirit of the Reformation but also the very heart of our penitent Christian faith. Those who believe it, share it.

Moreover, the Protestant pulpit has contributed more to individual freedom, spiritual growth, and conversion than we may realize. Preaching had almost ceased in the church of the sixteenth century. Few churches had pulpits and fewer still had pews. Worshipers stood or knelt to observe the transactions of a priest about a mysterious altar. Intelligible preaching was seldom heard.

There are those today who question the significance and power of preaching. Some feel that the modern preacher will soon be outmoded by rapidly developing media. It is worthy to note that history teaches that whenever preaching becomes apathetic or passes out of the church, society disintegrates and man plunges into despair. Preaching and religious progress have gone hand in hand. Every time a conscientious minister enters his pulpit, another reformation is in the making.

Protestantism revived the pulpit and gave the world the teachings of the Lord Jesus Christ through such mighty voices as Luther, Zwingli, Calvin, Knox, Wesley, Campbell, and scores of others. Protestantism has placed great faith in the pulpit and the dimensions of the pulpit have increased with the dedication of those in the pew. Protestants have never considered preaching as an end in itself, but only as a means of arousing the imagination and spiritual conviction—to convince man of his sin and call him to repentance and worship through the study of God's word, Christian fellowship, and service.

The preacher has sought to communicate the gospel. The minister is the monstrance of the message, he is not the message. In discussing the Christian minister, William Ellery Channing said, "Whilst directing men to the cross, he should speak as one who has prostrated himself at its foot. This is pulpit eloquence."[2]

Therefore we should not underestimate the prerogative of the Protestant to participate in a free society. The Reformers believed that since man was made in the image of God, he was able, worthy, and capable of making decisions. Under God he was free to choose everything, save the consequences of his acts. "Where the spirit of the Lord is, there is freedom." (2 Corinthians 3:17.)

Today, a frightful battle is raging for the minds and souls of men. The machine age has produced idleness, indifference, and many hours of leisure. Into this vacuum have moved mighty ideologies, some of which are sowing seeds of destruction. Pioneering in outer space seems more appealing than the shepherding of souls.

The threat of totalitarianism, wherever it appears and in whatever form, is contrary to the inalienable rights of the individual and the eternal rights of a Christian. Generally speaking, Communism is weakest where democracy is strongest. Communism has made slow progress in Protestant-dominated countries. Freedom is more than the absence of military police and political dictators. Freedom is a climate that favors personal development. But, as Reinhold Niebuhr has warned, "Man is most free in the discovery that he is not free." The

[2]Channing, *op. cit.*

individual is free to do only what is right. Society's freedom and effectiveness is dependent upon man's concept of and commitment to freedom. Protestantism believes in such freedom and endeavors to practice it.

As Protestants, ours is the prerogative to promote and demonstrate Christian unity. Whatever the tragedies and tyrannies of our time there is a tremendous sign of hope—the emerging sense of Christian togetherness. Everything points to increased co-operation between communions and religious bodies. Positive Protestantism embraces the ecumenical movement which now comprises some 170 different communions throughout the world. The genius of Christianity is oneness and wholeness. Before the cross, denominationalism is exceedingly inconsequential; commitment to Christ is all-important.

The ecumenical movement is a reformation in itself. In it are the seeds of revival; from it will come a revitalized Christianity.

Protestantism dies by itself. By nature it requires fellowship and reciprocal relations. We should heed the parable of the Samaritan Israelites. They were a sizeable group in Jesus' day and they often appear in his teachings. He told a parable about a good Samaritan. But today the Samaritans are within 300 of being extinct. This could well happen to any denomination that selfishly embraces its own work, will, and way to the exclusion of the larger fellowship.

A fire was consuming a church building. Members and neighbors sought to extinguish the flames. One man flippantly said, "This is the first time I ever saw you here"—to which the inactive church member replied, "This is the only time I ever saw the church on fire." The church of the Reformers was on fire. It was aflame with faith and dedication. Only this kind of church will consume the passion and greed of the hour and present to God a people without "spot or wrinkle." (Ephesians 5:27.)

If Protestantism is distressed, it is not because of external attacks, but because of the inertia and indifference of its own members. Individually and collectively, we are challenged to rise up and take our stand in this revolutionary day. The tides of men are moving and the church is challenged to bring the revolutionary ideas and desires of men within the Christian orbit. Christianity is the most dynamic of all revolutionary forces. It is essentially an invitation to start a one-man revolution. It must start with you and with me. Otherwise, Reformation Sunday is merely a celebration of past experiences rather than a courageous challenge to stand as *modern Reformers*.

The hour demands that we be worthy of the cross. This means that you and I must take, if necessary, unpopular positions in the community for the sake of the One who said, "I, when I am lifted up from the earth, will draw all men unto myself.'" (John 12:2.)

They Sought a Country

*By faith Abraham obeyed when he was called to go
out to a place which he was to receive as an inher-
itance; and he went out, not knowing where he was
to go.*

—Hebrews 11:8

T H A N K S G I V I N G   I S a distinctly American holiday.
It celebrates no birth, no battle, no anniversary of soldiers or
of statesmen. It is pre-eminently a condition of the heart, a pilgrimage into the ever-beckoning land of gratitude wherein
we are privileged to rethink, relive, and rededicate ourselves
to a way of life that catches up our heritage and our hopes.

Stephen Vincent Benét has trenchantly described the mighty
migration of our Founding Fathers in a narrative poem, *Western Star:*

There was a wind over England, and it blew.
(Have you heard the news of Virginia?)
A west wind blowing, the wind of a western star,
To gather men's lives like pollen and cast them forth,
Blowing in hedge and highway and seaport town,
Whirling dead leaf and living, but always blowing,
A salt wind, a sea wind, a wind from the world's end,
From the coasts that have new, wild names, from the huge unknown.[1]

[1]From *Western Star* by Stephen Vincent Benét. Rinehart & Company, Inc.
Copyright 1943 by Rosemary Carr Benét.

127

The founders of America were primarily explorers and the regions of their expeditions were not limited to the physical. They were evangels of high principle, dedicated to the proposition that all men have a responsible destiny. As Norman Cousins says, "The young American giants knew how to put men and ideas together. They connected their spiritual beliefs to political action. They saw no walls separating science, philosophy, religion, and art."[2]

Thanksgiving is so frequently associated with the Pilgrims that we forget there were other men of faith and thanksgiving.

The Jamestown Festival of 1957, celebrating America's three hundred fiftieth birthday, was a dramatic reminder of those who sought a country. Lest we should forget the stamina and spirit of those who established the first permanent English settlement in the New World, playwright Paul Green has recaptured the romance and ruggedness of those daring days in his drama, *The Founders.*

On December 20, 1606, three bold boats sailed down the Thames in London, searching for a safe port along the shores of Virginia. "Susan Constant," flagship of Sir Christopher Newport's fleet, 110' 7" long, was by far the largest vessel. Though she had only nineteen bunks, she carried fifty-four passengers and a crew of seventeen. She was a sturdy ship with the crudest of accommodations. No one had any privacy except the captain. There was no galley. When weather permitted, food was cooked in sand pots on deck.

The second largest ship in this history-making voyage was the "Godspeed." It was 69' 2" over all, and carried cramped sleeping quarters for twelve, yet she listed thirty-nine passengers and a crew of thirteen.

---

[2]*In God We Trust,* by Norman Cousins.   Copyright 1958 by Harper & Brothers. Used by permission.

Quite appropriately, one of the boats used by the Founders was the "Discovery." This small sailing ship displaced about twenty tons of water and measured 50′ 2¼″ from stem to stern. While aboard an authentic reproduction of the vessel, I was shocked to find it did not have full headroom and the rough "below" was partitioned for four bunks. Yet the "Discovery" brought over twelve passengers and a crew of nine. An inadvertent remark dropped by a tourist in our party lingers in my heart: "You certainly would have to believe in something, wouldn't you, to come across in this thing?"

"Yes," I replied, "you surely would. And they did."

It required one hundred twenty-eight days for the voyage. The Founders arrived at Cape Henry, Virginia, April 26, 1607, at four o'clock in the morning. On this windswept shore, the grateful settlers raised a "large wooden cross" and thanked God for their safe arrival. Jamestown was selected as their site on May 14. These were dark and daring days. The disease-infested swamps, together with Indian warfare, claimed many. Food was scarce. Several hundred colonists came to Virginia in the first six years of her founding, and at one point only sixty persons survived.

On June 7, 1610, it was decided to abandon the settlement. The colonists sailed down the James River once again to challenge the Atlantic. Next morning, Sir Thomas Gates, lieutenant governor of the colony, received word that Lord De la Warr had arrived at Point Comfort with settlers and supplies. It is said Governor Gates returned to the empty fort and, falling on his knees, thanked God the colony had been saved.

Nevertheless, the years that followed took their toll. At last, in 1619, Governor Sir George Yeardley called an assembly of the colonists in the Jamestown church. This was the first "representative legislature" attended in America. The House of

Burgesses in Williamsburg was to lay the foundations for our democratic way of life.

John Donne, dean of St. Paul's Cathedral and chaplain of the London Company, sponsor of the Jamestown expedition, said in his annual sermon (1622) to the Virginia Company, "You have made this Island, which is but the suburb of the Old World, a bridge and gallery to the New; to join all to that world that should never grow old, the Kingdom of Heaven."

Equally dramatic and significant is the story of the Pilgrims. On December 21, 1620, the voyaging "Mayflower" dropped anchor in Plymouth Bay. It had been a grueling voyage, taking the one-hundred-twenty-ton-capacity ship sixty-six days to make the perilous crossing. There had been disease, anxiety, and childbirth among 102 courageous passengers. Furthermore, they arrived on the bleak New England shore during a hard winter which ultimately claimed one-half of their number. However, when spring came and the captain of the "Mayflower" offered free passage to anyone desiring to return, not a single person accepted.

The fidelity of the forty-one mates who while still aboard the "Mayflower" had signed the famous Compact beginning with the words, "In the name of God, Amen," was taking on visible meaning. These chivalrous souls had dedicated themselves to the total causes of freedom. They had come to carve out a better way of life. Faith prompted the voyage; faith sustained the Pilgrims and their religious convictions constrained them to raise their voices in praise. Their hardships, sacrifice, devotion, concept of government, and vigorous religion all remind us of those who sought a country.

Jamestown, Yorktown, Williamsburg, Plymouth, Valley Forge, Philadelphia, Appomattox Court House, the Alamo—yea, every important place and event in our honored history reminds us that each generation has sought a country with ever-expanding horizons and deepening dimensions. Though physical frontiers are rapidly disappearing, there remain the dangerous borders of freedom and justice, brotherhood and good will, love and faith, which if adequately pursued will require the intelligence, fortitude, and faithfulness our Founding Fathers possessed.

America is not a completed country. Explorations and revolutions continue. Whereas it has grown to unprecedented greatness, we are facing today some of the most explosive and decisive issues in our history. The rights of free men are being challenged. Problems of church and state, missiles and men, loom before us in increasing proportions. Like Abraham, we are challenged to leave the communities of our own building to experience an undiscovered country of more perfect relationships and understandings.

Galileo with his telescope; Sir Isaac Newton with his theories of light and gravity; Benjamin Franklin with his printing shop and discoveries of electricity; Eli Whitney and his cotton gin; Robert Fulton and his steam engine; Florence Nightingale and her lamp of love; Bach and Beethoven with their ears tilted toward heaven; Luther and his faith; Webster and his words; Shakespeare and his poems; Jane Addams and Hull House; Roland Hayes and his voice; and George Washington Carver and the peanut—all these and countless others sought countries, stations of service, and expression for which we voice our praise and thanksgiving.

Christians the world over are challenged by the life of William Carey. This faithful British Baptist arrived in Calcutta in February, 1794. He proved his stature and spirit as a planter, linguist, and missionary-preacher. The days were hard and discouraging. For five years he did not win a single convert. For fourteen years he nursed a sick wife whose melancholy deepened into insanity. The pioneer work of this wonderful Christian gave an initiating impulse to world missions and the ecumenical movement. To stand in Carey's chapel and reflect on his faith is to remember his famous utterance: "Expect great things from God; attempt great things for God."

In 1857 a French research chemist named Louis Pasteur boldly announced that living organisms caused fermentation. It is claimed that this discovery opened "a thousand doors." Among other things it ultimately led to industrial chemistry and the manufacture of miracle drugs.

Orville and Wilbur Wright, proprietors of a bicycle shop in Dayton, Ohio, were interested in the problems of powered flight. Following the example of Lilienthal, they built and flew successfully unpowered gliders. Eventually they built a twelve-horsepower gasoline engine to power their glider. On December 17, 1903, at Kitty Hawk, North Carolina, the first heavier-than-air glider stayed aloft about twelve seconds. Later that same day, the amazing plane flew fifty-nine seconds and covered a distance of some 852 feet. That sandy runway at Kitty Hawk introduced the air age.

January 31, 1948, marks the date of the assassination of Mahatma Gandhi. He was on his way to prayer. Memorable comments were made around the world, but none more penetrating than Nehru's: "Light has gone out of our lives and there is darkness everywhere."

This spindly man who returned from South Africa to liberate his people is reminiscent of Moses. Although not comparable physically, they were kindred spirits. The man and the hour were matched. He was able to achieve in a single generation what diplomats, economists, and soldiers had pessimistically assigned to a distant future. Mahatma Gandhi sought a country in which to invest his life. Though dead, he continues to speak to multitudes who heard him gladly.

Coming closer to home, consider Dr. William Larimer Mellon, Jr., of the well-known and distinguished Pittsburgh family, who was so inspired by the work of Albert Schweitzer in Africa that he gave up his ranch in Arizona and, at an advanced age, turned back to school to study medicine. Today he and Mrs. Mellon head their own hospital in Haiti. Interestingly enough, the institution was named for Albert Schweitzer.

On December 2, 1942, a carefully selected group of twenty-two men under the leadership of the noted scientist, Arthur Compton, witnessed in an unsuspected laboratory beneath the west stands of Stagg Field, University of Chicago, the first nuclear fire. Since that historic moment, atom tests have blazed up around the world. Some fear the annihilation of man. Others hope for man's emancipation from the status of warrior to a more sincere worshiper of our wonderful Creator, God.

Arthur Compton, Erico Fermi, Walter Zinn, Herbert Anderson, and their colleagues sought a country, the climate of which only Christians can control.

On October 4, 1957, Russian scientists shocked the world with their moving moon rocket, Sputnik. The twenty-three-inch aluminum sphere weighed about one hundred eighty-four pounds and was filled with nitrogen, storage batteries, radio transmitters, and instruments to contact the earth. Calculations indicated that it circumnavigated the globe every ninety-six minutes. When news reached Paris of this miracle an observer commented: "The cost of this satellite is forty years of deprivations by the Russian people." Another quipped: "It is easier to make a revolution in the sky than on earth."

Cyclotrons have emerged as enticing cathedrals and the number of satellites in orbit determine a country's up-to-dateness and power over other nations.

Time would fail me to mention equally significant accomplishments of history. People of common acquaintance loom before us at this Thanksgiving season and we voice gratitude for their contributions to communal life. However, no memory is as fresh, no personality as challenging, as the Pilgrim of Galilee, who came preaching repentance and announcing that the kingdom of God was at hand. This Prophet understood the law and lore of his people, but he was not a prisoner of tradition nor of time. He respected the temple, but he sought a larger sanctuary wherein love was the altar and service the ritual. He gave himself in compassionate ministry to all types and conditions of men. He was the King of truth and the Lord of life whose judgments and teachings so disturbed the guardians of the *status quo* that he was killed.

The most condemning and compelling scene in all history is not Jamestown nor Plymouth Rock, but Calvary where Jesus of Nazareth died on his cross. Here was a man in search of a country—an undiscovered country, the kingdom of God—to which he bids us come.

On this day of remembrance and rededication to the best we know, let us enter into the joy of our Lord which is our strength and our hope. Let us "Praise God from whom all blessings flow." Above all, may we say "Thanks be to God for his inexpressible gift!" (2 Corinthians 9:15.)

The Pavilion of Women

. . . a woman who fears the Lord is to be praised.

—Proverbs 31:30b

I N   C E L E B R A T I N G   Woman's Day, Disciples of Christ emphasize the world outreach of the church. From the very beginning of their missionary movement, Disciples have recognized and honored the leadership of Christian women. Moreover, today we salute the named and unnamed, the honored and the unnoticed women of every generation and community who have heard the call of Christ and have endeavored to answer it in terms of Christian service.

The Pavilion of Women,[1] an exceedingly provocative novel, is germane to the occasion. As would be expected, its distinguished author, Pearl Buck, once again writes about China. The story concerns "a great family of the landed gentry through three generations." Madam Wu, heroine, celebrated her fortieth birthday. Life seemed to be losing its meaning. Although she had been married twenty-four years and was the mother of four sons, there was in her heart an indescribable emptiness. Hence she decided to withdraw from her life, and family responsibilities, and employed a concubine for her hus-

---

[1]*The Pavilion of Women*, by Pearl Buck. Adaptation used by permission of Harold Ober Associates, Inc.

band. The huge house suddenly became one of revolt and sin. Quickly the pavilion of sensuality became a pavilion of new power.

Brother André, Fengmo's tutor, was all but beaten to death by the notorious Green Band, "young ruffians who roamed the country roads and the city streets." The accident occurred when the kindly priest went to the rescue of a moneylender.

Upon hearing the distressing news, Madam Wu laid aside the conventional dignities associated with her class and hurried to the home of the foreign priest. He lived in the slums where derelicts and orphans and waifs found strange comradeship. The giant body of the beloved man lay on a narrow bamboo cot. Through the queue of milling onlookers the distinguished lady made her way to the bedside of the departing man. From a heart throbbing with emotion Madam Wu whispered, "I am here, tell me what I must do." With great difficulty the dying man said, "Feed my lambs." Death came quickly and with it a deluge of tears and compassionate calls from the children—"Father, Father!"

The concerned woman discovered that the priest had rented the once "haunted house" that beggars and foundlings might have a home. The words, "Feed my lambs," kept coming back through her troubled mind.

Now and with a sense of reality the words of her teacher lingered in her heart. Life was beginning to make sense. Brother André became to her the embodiment of the unseen God. By his stalwart and sacrificial life her witness now seemed frail and insignificant. With an awareness of her sins there came a resurgence of spirit and purpose. "My lambs!" They were his dirty children, twenty girls from the streets. In these frightened children Madam Wu could see the potentiality of lives coming to full flower. Now she understood it all.

The earthly possessions of the priest consisted of a cross, some books, one change of clothing and a crude telescope. But his spiritual ministry had converted a community—yes, the heart of a divided house. And with the delicacy of a great artist, Pearl Buck has the Chinese lady assume the funeral obligations of the priest. Then the spirit of reconciliation captured the great house. The children for whom the priest had cared were now Madame Wu's concern. The atmosphere was charged with the fragrance of faith. Fengmo returned from foreign study to become a rural schoolteacher. Ch'iuming, the first concubine, and Rulan, her daughter-in-law, went out as teachers. Conjure if you can the converted missionary— Madame Wu.

Pearl Buck has thoughtfully called her noval *The Pavilion of Women,* thus permitting our imagination to roam over some of the women of the Bible who dwell under the pavilion of the Most High.

At the mention of such a pavilion Mary, the mother of Jesus, comes to mind. Our Roman Catholic friends have deified her and thus made her an object of worship. We cannot and dare not go that far. But certainly we need a greater appreciation for the Mother of our Lord and to recognize a bit more clearly her place in the pavilion of women.

The late John Erskine declared that the human life of Jesus began with a revelation to Mary. "She had a dream for her child." Disassociate prejudice from your mind. Remember no more the poor pictures you have seen of the Madonna and try to visualize her as a simple peasant girl scarcely more than eighteen years of age with ruddy cheeks. Her bone was heavy and her hands rough from toil. She was an unspoiled, unsophisticated girl whose heart was as pure as her body.

Mary was betrothed to a neighboring man, Joseph. According to tradition he was considerably her senior and when he discovered she was with child, he was troubled and embarrassed. But, the Gospel of Matthew records, he like Mary was assured in a dream that the child was of God.

Mary was a watchful, loving mother. Although she did not understand her remarkable Son, she was patient and prayerful. She followed his development with pride and his ministry with faith. Mary knew of his travels and of his teachings. She heard of his trial. She stood by him at the cross. Jesus saw Mary and saluted her. John took her to his home.

Rose Trumbull knew something of Mary's place in the Christian world and in the pavilion of great women when she wrote:

> Mary, when that little child
>   Lay upon your heart at rest,
> Did the thorns, Maid-mother mild,
>   Pierce your breast?
>
> Mary, when that little child
>   Softly kissed your cheek benign,
> Did you know, O Mary mild,
>   Judas' sign?
>
> Mary, when that little child
>   Cooed and prattled at your knee,
> Did you see with heartbeat wild,
>   Calvary?[2]

Through the door of retrospect let us look at another pioneering, sacrificial soul. Her name is Lydia and she lived in Philippi. The ancient city stood in the southeast corner of Macedonia, famed as the scene of battle between Anthony

---

[2]"Mary," from *Masterpieces of Religious Verse*. Reprinted by permission of Harper & Brothers.

and Octavius and Brutus and Cassius in the year 42 B.C. It was here that the Apostle Paul preached, perhaps for the first time in Europe. Services were conducted outside the city gates, along the river's edge. A distinguished business lady, "a dealer in purple," was in that little congregation. God warmed her heart and she was converted. After she and her household were baptized she said to her new colleagues: "'If you have judged me to be faithful to the Lord, come to my house and stay.'" (Acts 16:15.)

Lydia was a businesswoman dealing in purple cloth. The assumption is she operated a rather fine fabric shop. But under the influence of the Christian message she became a dealer in the royalties of God and her home was converted into a dormitory for God's workers. Originally Lydia dealt in purple cloth. Now she dealt with the fabric of human lives. The royal priesthood of God found sanctuary in her soul.

The names of Ruth and Esther, Mary and Martha, Dorcas and Phoebe all rush to mind. Joan of Arc, Susanna Wesley, Florence Nightingale, Edith Cavell and Jane Addams, all kindle memories. In our own day such wonderful women as Muriel Lester, Mrs. Theodore O. Wedel, Mrs. Harper Sibley, Madame Chiang Kai-shek, Eleanor Roosevelt, and Mrs. James D. Wyker, to mention only a few, are witnesses to great living.

As we consider the great women of the ages, we must not lose sight of the young struggling mothers who have always contributed so much to the character of Christianity. Some of these wonderful mothers are working to supplement the family income, others are working because they enjoy it; still others labor for God amid the noise, care, and responsibility of those who tug at their skirts.

Moreover, who could calculate the invaluable contribution of women to the World Church? We marvel at the work of United Church Women with approximately 2,000 state and local councils which represent more than 10,000,000 Christian women. The emphasis they place on prayer, love offerings, and fellowship is reminiscent of the early church.

Furthermore, let us not lose sight of the economic status and influence of women. As never before in history women occupy positions of authority and prominence. Marthann H. Voss has set forth astounding facts about today's women. They own seventy per cent of this country's wealth, forty per cent of all real estate, possess fifty per cent of the stock in industrial corporations, are beneficiaries of eighty per cent of all life insurance, spend about eighty-five per cent of the family income and have much to say about what should be done with the rest. Women carry the principal responsibility for youth education. They have ninety-two labor-saving devices, which help them have more time than any previous generation. Furthermore, American women make up sixty-five per cent of our church membership.[3]

Today we think not only of church women but also of the world outreach of the church. If there was ever a time when the Christian family needs to exert itself, it is now. No longer can one member of the family study and support missions. The task is too great. The family and the church must unite zestfully in sharing and supporting the pavilion of missions, so often carried virtually alone by women.

The end of war has not brought peace, only the opportunity to serve. David Lawrence and others have reminded us that war—past, present and future—is a major factor in our present uneasy economy. Countless million of souls in Europe and Asia are facing a tidal wave of uncertainty.

[3]See *Stewardship Facts*, Arthur O. Rinden, Editor, published by Department of Stewardship and Benevolence, National Council of Churches in the U. S. A., 257 Fourth Avenue, New York 10, N. Y., p. 9.

Here at home the Department of Justice continues to shock us with statistics. Juvenile delinquency and adult deterioration are ever before us. In the next twelve months 1,000,000 boys and girls under twenty-one years of age will commit crimes serious enough for them to be picked up by the police. Yet we are advised that for every one apprehended, perhaps three will escape. Every two minutes, a car is stolen in America and one-half of them by youths under seventeen. Currently we are spending $1.60 on crime for every $1.00 spent on education. Furthermore we are advised that at least 100,-000 children are born out of wedlock in our country each year. America also needs the church.

In such a sordid world we must be certain that men as well as women understand and participate in the outreach program of the church. As we face stupendous programs for world order and peace, dare we rely on the willing but inadequate support given missionary organizations? No. The time has come for every believer in humanity, every worshiper of God to say, "His royal pavilion must cover the earth."

Dean Hodges of Cambridge once declared the great days of the church were those of the "missionaries, monks, and Methodists." If you investigate these periods of history you will discover they were days when the laity of the church manifested an unbelievable loyalty and demonstrated a contagious stewardship.

Woman's Day is a challenge to think magnificently of missions. Christians are asked to visualize the yeast of the Spirit working in every heart and home throughout the world. This means that you and I must become missionaries in the communities where we live.

Hulda Niebuhr shares an experience from the schoolroom of Alice Humphreys. On a rainy Monday at recess when the children were forced to remain indoors, the teacher listened to the fascinating conversations of the children. They were discussing their churches. One child, reflecting on the conversations, quietly said, "I didn't see who took Jesus home." The teacher was alert as she watched the matter-of-fact reaction of her class. Nonchalantly, they asked, "Who would have taken him home?" Little Kathie immediately said, "It would have been Old Barney." Old Barney had hardly lived the life of a Sunday school teacher. However, he was fond of the children and was always doing small favors for them. The children recognized deeds rather than pious professions.

Today, as well as every Sunday, the Lord Jesus asks, "Who will take me home, and to the homes of those who know me not?" A missionary, whether at home or abroad, takes Christ to God's children by his deeds of love.

Creighton Lacy, professor of missions at Duke University Divinity School, tells of an African woman who walked fifty miles to a mission hospital for treatment. The doctors were amazed and asked, "Why did you come so far, when the road from your home went right by a government hospital? Don't you know the medicines are the same?"

"Oh, yes," the dear woman replied, "the medicines are the same, but the hands are different."[4]

---

[4]From "You Must Be a Missionary," by Creighton Lacy. Copyrighted by the Christian Century Foundation and reprinted by permission of *The Pulpit* from the issue of January, 1958.

The Bible through the Years

*"The people who sat in darkness
have seen a great light."*
—*Matthew 4:16*

T H E   B I B L E is our common heritage and contains our common hope. It is an inexhaustible resource for every conceivable situation and has been tested and refined by the wisdom of the centuries. Communions differ in their theology and procedures of worship. Churches vary in their conception of the Christian ministry. Doctrines of the churches provoke debate. The vocabulary and ritual of Christians are as dissimilar as are the requirements for church membership. But, however varied its use and interpretation, all Christians cherish the Bible.

Holy Scripture is not a divine "fall-out." Whereas Moslems believe that the Koran mysteriously appeared in finished form and the Mormons maintain that the Book of Mormon was uniquely delivered to Joseph Smith, Christians make no such claim for the Bible. Reverently they recall its rise and reception.

The Christian recognizes the ancient setting of the Bible lands and interprets the literature accordingly. Although the Bible is largely the product of a single nation, the beloved and continuing community of God; it was, nevertheless, written, collected, and edited by individuals. The process of composing the Bible approximated a thousand years.

One might well ask, "How did we get our Bible?" Much of the material in the Old Testament belongs to what scholars call "the preliterary or oral period" of history. Ancient storytellers were wonderfully adept in the art of transmitting information, especially their own history, from one generation to another. Until about 1000 B.C. the ancient traditions were so transmitted.

About a half century later, a scribe or a group of scribes compiled stories of the tribes in Southern Palestine. Ultimately this material was known as the "J document." It was a writing down of the oral tradition, containing songs, poems, and history. In due time, the Northern tribes broke away from Judah and became an independent kingdom. Afterward, about 750 B.C., another writer, or group of writers, offered a history centering on the Northern tribes. This material is usually identified as the "E document." Several decades later, the Northern Kingdom fell before the armies of Assyria. The E material was taken by refugees into Judah and ultimately became incorporated into the J document in what is called "JE."

About a century later, in 621 B.C., Judah, the Southern Kingdom, was in a religious relapse. While repairs were being made to the temple, a manuscript, part of the Book of Deuteronomy, was discovered. Before long Deuteronomy (often abbreviated to D) was joined to J and E.

Approximately a century after the Babylonian exiles returned to Palestine, there occurred a major political and religious reform under the leadership of Nehemiah (444 B.C.) and Ezra (398 B.C.). Out of this emerged a considerable quantity of priestly legislation as well as a considerable revision of the ancient traditions from a priestly point of view. This material was fused with the JED material of the Pentateuch. Thus, scholars often speak of the Pentateuch as being composed of "JEDP."

In the fourth century B.C. the Pentateuch was accepted as the standard by which Jews were to fulfill their obligations to God and to man. Editors rather than authors are responsible for its present form.

Many other composite books were to follow. The Book of Psalms was the hymnal of ancient Israel. Proverbs was probably used as a textbook by aspiring young men. Meanwhile other books were being written. Thus, by about 200 B.C., the majority of the Old Testament scrolls were completed.

As we have indicated, the first five books of the Old Testament were classified as the Pentateuch or the Law. The second centered around the prophets and historical accounts, while the remaining works were simply referred to as the "writings." The material was being used more and more, so at the Palestinian village of Jamnia, A.D. 90-100, a council of rabbis formally adopted what the Jewish community had already accepted. Thus, the text of what now comprises the thirty-nine books of our Old Testament was completed. We are told that it required all of 1100 years to compose, collect, compile, and edit the Old Testament. It became the standard of living and worship not only for ancient Jews, but also for early Christians.

"The story of the New Testament," says M. Jack Suggs, "begins with a man who wrote no part of it but was responsible for all of it."[1] In contrast to the centuries required to produce the Old Testament, the New Testament was more than likely written and collected in little over a century. It may come as a surprise that the earliest writings in the New Testament are not the Gospels but the Epistles of Paul. First Thessalonians is said to be the earliest of all, dating back to about A.D. 50. The Pauline letters directed to specific churches and people were brought together to form what we now call Epistles. Mark is the earliest Gospel and was written from Rome around A.D. 70.

A heretic named Marcion advanced the false notion that the Old and New Testaments represented different "Gods" and consequently gave himself to the task of determining "safe writings." He proceeded to exclude the Old Testament and much of the New. However, his aggressiveness stimulated the early Church to examine and produce its own literature. By the year A.D. 200, the Gospels, Acts of the Apostles, and Paul's writings were accepted as the basic written authority for the Christian community. Other books were pending acceptance. By A.D. 367, the twenty-seven books that comprise our New Testament were recognized by the early Church. These writings were referred to as the "Canon," since they were and are accepted as the standard of Christian living and faith.

Communication was, and continues to be, a challenging problem. Unless one hears in his own tongue, he does not completely understand. The problem of translating the books was imperative. The Old Testament was composed mainly in Hebrew, although some books were written in part or wholly in Aramaic and the New Testament in Greek. Very early the Old Testament had been translated into Greek and the Bible of the earliest Christians was in Greek.

By the third century the church had already moved into areas where Greek was not understood. The Word had to be translated into national tongues. The foremost biblical scholar of his day, Jerome, at the request of Pope Damascus, revised the many old Latin versions. This tremendous contribution was accomplished in Bethlehem and the translation is known as the Vulgate, meaning "common" tongue of the people. It was not until long after the Middle Ages that the average man could read. Priests and other well-educated men were the exception. Scholars in the following centuries contributed several partial and complete translations of the Scriptures in different languages.

John Wycliffe and his colleagues using the text of Jerome produced the first complete English translation of the Bible in 1382. Wycliffe's translation was a lasting contribution to Christendom.

William Tyndale, another translator, developed his work from the original languages. He also received help from Martin Luther's translation of 1522. He carried his English manuscript into Germany where Johann Gutenberg printed it. Copies of his New Testament were smuggled back to England in bales of cotton. Later, Tyndale was seized by authorities of Charles V and thrown into prison. He was tried for heresy and condemned to death. Among his last words were: "Lord, open thou the King of England's eyes." His translation of 1525 as well as Wycliffe's incited many reforms.

Miles Coverdale, who derived much help from Tyndale's translation, produced a complete English edition of the Bible in 1535. Thus, the language barrier was transcended and believers heard in their own tongue.

Many English translations followed including the Great Bible of 1539, the Geneva Bible of 1560, and the Bishop's Bible of 1568. However, the most notable was the Authorized Version commonly called the King James Version. The king who came to the throne of England in 1603 appointed fifty-four scholars to bring out a new version based on the original languages. In 1611 these commissioned revisers produced a new Bible.

It is probably not very widely known that there were at least seventy "private versions" of the Bible or of notable parts thereof produced by members of various Protestant groups between the Authorized Version of 1611 and the Revised Version of 1881-85.[2]

Notwithstanding the excellence and beauty of the King James Version, it was felt that with newly discovered manuscripts, a more accurate and understandable rendering of the Scriptures was needed. Translators of the King James New Testament worked with only eight major manuscripts; perhaps the oldest was a tenth-century document. Present-day scholars have access to archaeological materials hitherto unknown and about 4,500 Greek manuscripts, some dating back to the third, fourth, and fifth centuries. The most-discussed discovery of recent years is, of course, the Dead Sea Scrolls. One of the Hebrew manuscripts dates from between the first and second centuries B.C.

A committee of the foremost biblical scholars in the country, headed by Luther A. Weigle, gave fourteen years to the production of the Revised Standard Version. The New Testament appeared in 1946 and the complete Bible in 1952. Thus, today we have the living Word in familiar, accurate, and modern language.

Today the Bible appears in more than 1,100 tongues. It is estimated that ninety-seven per cent of the peoples of the world now have access to the Book of books in their own language.

Ours is a day of books. Some 525,393,000 volumes exclusive of textbooks and encyclopedias were sold in the United States in 1956.[3] About 12,000 new titles appear each year; yet the Bible continues to lead the way in practically every area of

---

[2]From "English Versions since 1611," by Father Sebastian Bullough, O.P., in *The Bible Today*. Copyright 1955 by Harper & Brothers. Used by permission.
[3]See *Publisher's Weekly*, September 16, 1957.

nonfiction publication. This in itself is a testimony to the unconquerable light of the centuries.

The uniqueness of the Bible is in the extraordinary way it speaks to every man. In the words of Pope Gregory the Great, "The Bible is a stream wherein the elephant may swim and the lamb may wade." Any mind may approach it and all minds find satisfaction therein.

The Bible has survived the fires of the ages, the angers of men, and the attitudes of its readers. It has been the foundation upon which nations have flourished and individuals have found faith in God. During Queen Victoria's reign a Prince of India inquired of England's glory. The Queen sent him a Bible, inscribing on its flyleaf, "This Book is the source of England's glory."

The Bible is the foundation on which the nation which would endure must rest. This is true of America. Our Founding Fathers lived by the Bible. The language of the Bible found its way into the Charter and the Constitution. It was the principal textbook used by children of the Puritan settlers, and the early colleges of our land were started to perpetuate its teachings. No one, perhaps, has expressed more succinctly the place of the Bible in our nation than did President Jackson: "That Book, sir, is the rock on which our Republic rests."

If you like biography, you will find nothing to surpass the lives of the stalwarts etched in this spiritual Thesaurus. If you enjoy travel, read of the Hebrew heroes. If you prefer tracing growing institutions and insights, read the account of government and law in Exodus or re-examine the Ten Commandments. If you like poetry, explore the Book of Psalms. Its rhythmic beauty is unexcelled. There is no lovelier sentence in all literature than: "The Lord is my Shepherd, I shall not want." If you prefer pathos, turn to the Book of Job. The Book of Ruth is a picture of romance and love. The Gospels and the Epistles of Paul send the Lord Christ walking through your heart.

To the man of faith the Bible is the bread of life.

Whatever you need to develop in your life, read the Bible. It may be embarrassing, for its truth is impartial. The Bible is not a primer of science, rather a handbook for living. It reveals heavenly wisdom and a God of infinite love.

How should you read the Bible? Should you read it as you would any other book, beginning with the first page? I think not. Since some portions of the Book are easier to read than others, perhaps it would be more helpful to begin with one of the Gospels, Mark for example, and then turn to the history of the early Church in The Acts of the Apostles. Read the Epistles of Paul. Read as a discipline. Read as a devotion. Read to find yourself. Read to find God's will for your life. Read until you find yourself in the eternal plan.

To read and use the Bible intelligently, you must remember that it has its own history. Therefore, if you are to derive the maximum help, you must be familiar with the setting and the occasion of the particular book or section. You must also become familiar with some of the commentaries and books of Bible orientation.

In *The Modern Use of the Bible,* Dr. Fosdick declares there are at least four ways in which to use the Bible: You may acquaint yourself with its "beauty spots" and quote them verbatim; you may know its individual books; and you may have an understanding of its principal characters. All this is important. However, he says, "Only as a man is able to trace up through the whole Scripture the development of its structure and ideas does he really know the Bible." He continues by suggesting that no one knows the Bible until he stumbles upon himself on its pages.

A critic of Billy Graham's New York crusade said: "All he does is to hold up the Bible and shout!" This comment, of course, is capable of more than one interpretation. Positively speaking, however, what more could an evangelist, indeed any Christian, do than hold up the eternal principles and teachings of the Bible, especially the life of the One who fulfilled it?

On Universal Bible Sunday, let us join Sara E. Taylor in voicing our thanksgiving for the divine gift:

> O God of Light, Thy word, a lamp unfailing,
> Shines through the darkness of our earthly way,
> O'er fear and doubt, o'er black despair prevailing,
> Guiding our steps to Thine eternal day.
>
> From days of old, through swiftly rolling ages,
> Thou hast revealed Thy will to mortal men,
> Speaking to saints, to prophets, kings, and sages,
> Who wrote the message with immortal pen.
>
> Undimmed by time, the Word is still revealing
> To sinful men Thy justice and Thy grace;
> And questing hearts that long for peace and healing
> See Thy compassion in the Saviour's face.
>
> To all the world the message Thou art sending,
> To every land, to every race and clan;
> And myriad tongues, in one great anthem blending,
> Acclaim with joy Thy wondrous gift to man.[4]

---

[4]From *Ten New Bible Hymns*. Copyright 1952, by the Hymn Society of America; used by permission.

On Going to Bethlehem

"Let us go over to Bethlehem and see this thing that has happened, which the Lord has made known to us."

—*Luke 2:15*

W E   D R O V E   F R O M   Jerusalem to Bethlehem, ordinarily a distance of about six miles, but because of the Palestinian partition, the circuitous route now covers approximately twelve miles. Upon reaching the quaint town nestled in the corrugated Judean hills, we went immediately to the Church of the Nativity. Externally and physically, the stone structure, built in the shape of a cross, resembles a bastion more than a house of worship. It is now jointly used by Catholics, Greek Orthodox, and Armenian Christians. The shrine is entered through an unusually small door.

However, once the threshold of the church is crossed, the atmosphere is charged by an invisible Presence. A courteous caretaker gave slender candles to those who wished them. With these lighted tapers we made our way down winding steps to the Grotto and the sacred spot where tradition says Christ was born. Our small company, which included an Arab guide, an Orthodox priest, and a soldier from Sudan, encircled the Altar of the Magi. I stood by the dark soldier. There was a moment of silence: sober, searching silence. The fondest memories and venerations of the ages united us. Then in different voices, even languages, we sang, "Silent Night, Holy Night." There was not a dry eye in the crowd. By the calendar it was September, but our hearts said it was Christmas.

What a place for the Savior of the world to be born: no central heating, no germicidal lamp to purify the air for the God-given Baby, no pediatrician to prescribe the precise formula, or nurse to administer medical needs. In fact the only certainty in that cattle cave was the presence of Almighty God.

As I stood in that hallowed spot, the centuries spoke; scrolls of history unrolled before me as I recalled more vividly some of the ancient pilgrims who had gone to Bethlehem. In Genesis we read the remarkable romance of Jacob and Rachel. When the trickster in exile first saw Rachel, she was standing by a well. Immediately, he loved her. Eventually Jacob made known to Rachel's father his desire to marry her. And for seven years he labored for the hand and heart of Rachel—only to receive her older sister, Leah. Then an additional seven years was demanded by Laban for Rachel. Jacob acquiesced. At last, after the consummation of their marriage, the birth of Joseph, and the accumulation of flocks, they turned homeward. Near Ephrathah, Bethlehem, Rachel died in childbirth.

Bethlehem was for Jacob a burial ground. Halfway between the city of David and Jerusalem he built a sepulchre in memory of Rachel. This remarkable tomb still stands as a shrine to love. Jacob and Rachel preceded Joseph and Mary to Bethlehem. To the former, it was death; to the anointed, it was life.

Ruth and Naomi also went to the "little town of Bethlehem." In fact, Naomi was born there. However, the pinch of famine drove her to Moab. While living on this tableland east of the Dead Sea, Naomi lost through death both her husband and her sons who had married Moabite women. With the burdens of sorrow and destitution weighing heavily upon her heart, Naomi decided to return to Bethlehem and so bade farewell to her daughters-in-law. Orpah seemed content to say, "Good-bye," but not Ruth. In one of the greatest confessions of love ever recorded she said, "Entreat me not to leave you or to return from following you; for where you go I will go, and where you lodge I will lodge; your people shall be my people, and your God my God; where you die I will die, and there will I be buried." (Ruth 1:16-17.)

So the women journeyed to Bethlehem and when they entered the city the neighbors cried out, asking, "Is this Naomi?" She said to them, "Do not call me Naomi, call me Mara, for the Almighty has dealt very bitterly with me. I went away full, and the LORD has brought me back empty." (Ruth 1:19-21.) There Ruth met Boaz and their love culminated in a happy family.

David, the grandson of Naomi, frequently went to Bethlehem. He was reared just outside the village. This "ruddy" and courageous youth set the Philistines to flight with his sling and stone. David killed Goliath their champion. When the unusual young man was selected king, the Bethlehemites were proud to say, "The new king is from our town!" Indeed, he loved Bethlehem and it is often called "the city of David."

Micah, the Hebrew prophet, who lived 700 years and more before Christ, visited Bethlehem. His was a strange mission. The seer journeyed to the city of David to say,

But you, O Bethlehem Ephrathah,
    who are little to be among the clans of Judah,
from you shall come forth for me
    one who is to be ruler in Israel,

whose origin is from of old,
    from ancient days.

—Micah 5:2

As I fed on these and other sacred memories, the record of
that wondrous night filled my heart with heavenly awe. The
calculations of the wise men seemed more phenomenal; the
vision of the shepherds more prophetic and compelling. To
think that in the fullness of time God had chosen Bethlehem,
of all places in the world, obscure and inaccessible, as the
birthplace of his Son and to think that I, too, was privileged
to stand where tradition says he was born, was all very wonderful.

To be with Jesus in Bethlehem was to experience a new understanding of Christmas. It was to realize with clearer certainty that heaven had touched the "earth with gladness" and
that God had uniquely and permanently invaded the heart of
man. Though surrounded by competing faiths, in Bethlehem
one forgets the theological intricacies of the incarnation and is
reassured that the Word has been fleshed. Christmas becomes
a personal invitation to meet the King of kings and not the
clowns of commercialism.

Such an experience reminds one of the poetical picture of
Nancy Hanks presented by Rosemary Benét. In her imagination she visualizes Nancy returning to earth seeking information concerning her child. Among other pensive queries she
asks,

Where's my son?
What's he done?
Did he grow tall?
Did he learn to read?
Did he get to town?[1]

---

[1]*Nancy Hanks* by Rosemary Carr Benét. From *A Book of Americans*. Rinehart
& Company, Inc. Copyright 1933 by Rosemary and Stephen Vincent Benét.

It is a tenderly touching poem. Nancy Hanks never knew—or did she?—that her son grew strong, as strong as justice and as straight as a woodsman's wedge.

She never knew—or did she?—that he learned to read the printed word and to courageously perform the correct deed.

Nancy Hanks never knew—or did she?—that the boy whom she left at nine, went to town, the big town of Washington, D. C., in the most crucial hours of his country's history and left a monument not only in marble but also in the memories of men as the great watershed of justice, a giant of righteousness.

Abraham Lincoln reached a rare maturity.

Christmas, then, when seen through the prisms of Bethlehem, presents a picture of another boy who grew up to be a Man—God's only begotten Son. His mother, Mary, saw him develop though she understood him not. She listened to his sermons but she could not fully comprehend them. She stood by his cross but she could not see the open tomb.

It seems to me that one of the tragedies of Christmas is that we continue to worship a Baby Jesus. In fact, too many of us are still in the nursery with rhyme and song. We are too often Teddy-bear Christians. The greater message of Christmas is that this Baby, who uniquely invaded the world, grew up to be the Savior of mankind. His devastating courage and eternal life compel the world to visit Bethlehem, the starting place in the celestial journey.

Christmas is primarily a pilgrimage from where we are to where God would have us be—Bethlehem. Though all may not be privileged to visit the sacred shrine, we are privileged to open our minds and our hearts to his coming. There is room for all in the Bethlehem stall.

Let the sorrowful, like Jacob, visit Bethlehem and find solace for their harrowed hearts in the knowledge that the One born there was burdened with sorrow and acquainted with grief—yet triumphantly exclaimed, "In the world you have tribulation; but be of good cheer, I have overcome the world." (John 16:33.)

Let laborers, people who earn their living with their hands and who are constantly caught in public pressures, visit Bethlehem and meet the Carpenter who lifted labor to the level of worship.

Let the farmer who toils between the dust of the clod and the heat of the sun, go to Bethlehem and reclaim his kinship with the shepherds who, in their faithful vigil, saw the star, recognized its brilliance and followed its rays confidently, saying, "Let us go over to Bethlehem and see this thing that has happened, which the Lord has made known to us."

Let lovers go to Bethlehem and, like Ruth and Boaz, start life anew, forgetting the shambles of the past and, laying hold with fresh hope to the promises of tomorrow, begin again.

Let businessmen also make the journey and discover afresh that all men, irrespective of station or skill, are commissioned to look after our Father's business.

Let professional men and women visit the altar of birth and commune with the Great Physician, examining once again their own professions.

Let churchmen go to Bethlehem and join the prophets and wise men in finding justification for their faith.

Let every man and woman and child in all the world join in the mighty pilgrimage to Bethlehem, marching to the rhythmic assurances of the ages and to angel song, "For to you is born this day in the city of David a Savior, who is

Christ the Lord." (Luke 2:11.) Let our hearts rejoice in the knowledge that faith in the Bethlehem miracle is essential to an understanding of the miracle of the cross.

Man needs to relive the events that occurred in Bethlehem and in Jerusalem. They are twin cities! Man needs the hope that this Palestinian Preacher announced to the world. Man needs the security of the cross; the faith of the open tomb. Christmas is a pilgrimage to Jerusalem via Bethlehem. There we must tarry by the ancient cross and rethink and recommit ourselves to Paul's declaration: "For the love of Christ controls us, because we are convinced that one has died for all; therefore all have died. And he died for all, that those who live might live no longer for themselves but for him who for their sake died and was raised." (2 Corinthians 5:14-15.)

> "How far is it to Bethlehem town?"
> Just over Jerusalem hills adown,
> Past lovely Rachel's white-domed tomb—
> Sweet shrine of motherhood's young doom.
>
> It isn't far to Bethlehem town—
> Just over the dusty roads adown,
> Past Wise Men's well, still offering
> Cool draughts from welcome wayside spring;
> Past shepherds with their flutes of reed
> That charm the woolly sheep they lead;
> Past boys with kites on hilltops flying,
> And soon you're there where Bethlehem's lying
> Sunned white and sweet on olived slopes,
> Gold-lighted still with Judah's hopes.
>
> And so we find the Shepherd's field
> And plain that gave rich Boaz yield;
> And look where Herod's villa stood.

We thrill that earthly parenthood
Could foster Christ who was all-good;
And thrill that Bethlehem town today
Looks down on Christian homes that pray.

It isn't far to Bethlehem town!
It's anywhere that Christ comes down
And finds in people's friendly face
A welcome and abiding place.
The road to Bethlehem runs right through
The homes of folks like me and you.[2]

---

[2]"How Far to Bethlehem," by Madelaine Miller.

The Peril of Not Looking Back

"Look to the rock from which you were hewn,
and to the quarry from which you were digged."

—*Isaiah 51:1*

I N M Y S E N I O R year in seminary there came one of those never-to-be-forgotten experiences. I was home for Christmas and Father suggested that we drive up-country to visit the place of his birth. We drove as far as possible, then parked the car and walked to the site of the old homestead.

Weeds claimed the place. Although the years had wrought many changes, Father seemed perfectly at home as he described the scene of his childhood. I sensed a tenderness in his voice and a great pride in his heart. At last he said, "I would like to drink from the old spring." He found a trace of the path and followed it to the spring branch. Kneeling, he brushed the leaves aside, and drank from the hallowed stream. Then I followed him in the ritual.

Father was obviously deeply moved—and so was I—for in turning back to the old place, he was not only leading me over ancestral ground, but he was also reliving a happy childhood. He told me things about our kinsmen which I had never heard before. In looking back with Father, I gained a new perspective of our family which continues to be satisfying and challenging.

We are constantly admonished to look ahead and are advised that "the best is yet to be." Sermons at this season of the year are apt to spring from animated texts. Among them: " 'Tell the people of Israel to go forward.' " (Exodus 14:15.) "Forgetting what lies behind and straining forward . . . I press on. . ." (Philippians 3:13.) " 'No one who puts his hand to the plow and looks back is fit for the kingdom of God.' " (Luke 9:62.) Then the classic story of Lot's wife who, upon looking back, turned into a "pillar of salt" is frequently cited. (Genesis 19:26.)

However essential the forward look may be, progress is frequently dependent upon an understanding and appreciation of one's heritage. Mistakes are not committed in the future, only in the present. And we are very stupid indeed when we ignore our mistakes and refuse to consult the past. On the eve of his return to Judea from Babylonian exile, the second Isaiah said to his contemporaries, "Look to the rock from which you were hewn, and to the quarry from which you were digged." The prophet admonished his people to reminisce, to rethink their lineage that they might fully appreciate their situation and intelligently plan for the future. Some of the Israelites had grown old both in years and in hope and they needed the encouraging words of the prophet.

To deny the necessity of retrospective analysis is to live recklessly in the present without due regard for the past. In discussing scientific experience, Elton Trueblood says, "Our knowledge of any event in Nature is not complete until we know the reason for the event."[1] This is likewise true of most

---

[1]David Elton Trueblood, *Philosophy of Religion*, New York: Harper and Brothers, 1957, p. 105.

experiences. Thus, as we stand in the shadows of this year, we do well to look back over the road we have traveled lest we stumble forward in fear and frustration. From our present vantage point, perplexing events may seem clearer.

Is it too early to suggest that we look back at Christmas? The important question is not, What did you get for Christmas, but What did you give at Christmas? It is relatively easy to answer the first part of this concern. Any chattering child will tell you what Santa Claus brought him. But the latter part of the question is more difficult. Unless Christmas has left a deposit of genuine love in our lives, unless we have been blessed rather than financially bled by the experience, this was just another costly and enervating holiday. Unless we have given the best of self and substance to Christ, we have been parasites and not pilgrims to Bethlehem.

As we contemplate the first Christmas—and how poor would be our faith if we did not look back to the miracle of Bethlehem—we immediately discover that those who experienced Christmas received something wonderful and abiding. "The shepherds returned, glorifying and praising God." (Luke 2: 20.) A miracle had taken place. There was praise upon their lips and prayer and victory in their hearts as they went back to the desolate hillsides with hope.

Mary and Joseph were inarticulate. Matthew tells us that, being warned of God in a dream, the wise men returned home another way. They were overwhelmed with awe. Learning of Herod's wrath, Mary and Joseph sought refuge in Egypt. Did you receive anything from Christmas that enabled you to go home a different way—in the same car perhaps, and to the familiar job, but with different concerns and new convictions? Did Christmas hang a new star in your sky?

Dr. Van Kirk tells of a little girl who was standing with her mother on a street corner following a shower. Suddenly bright sunlight pierced the clouds. The alert child noticed a small puddle of water with a shimmer of oil making it iridescent. She immediately exclaimed, "Mother, there's a rainbow gone to smash!" Christmas brings God's spiritual rainbow out of heaven and places it at your feet. Did Christmas go to smash in selfishness and crowded schedules, or did it lead you to a guiding star?

"Look to the rock from which you were hewn and to the quarry from which you were digged."

In quoting this sentence from Second Isaiah one is challenged to examine his personal study and application of God's Word. The Bible is the sacred rock from which our principles and philosophies of life, fortitude, and faith are hewn. It speaks of God's kingdom. As we approach the year's end, let us look back with open and inquisitive minds to this quarry of indestructible truth. Has your Bible opened and closed enough this year? Has it been a beacon of light and inspiration or a battleground of debate and doubt?

The Bible is the record of divine revelation culminating in Jesus Christ, the abiding Word. Realistically speaking, the Bible makes no attempt to present a reasoned theology. In robust fashion it reveals man's encounter with God and God's dealings with man. The Bible presents the witness of prophets and apostles. It is a book of spiritual discovery. As Dr. Hendrick Kraemer of the World Council of Churches has said, "In the deepest possible sense, the Bible is the book of the Church." It has much to say about sin and death, thus it is qualified to speak about life. The central theme of the Bible is Immanuel—"God with us."

Do you read the Bible like the headlines? Do you read the Bible like any other book? Dr. Nels Ferré correctly asserts, "The Bible is read rightly only when we meet God through it."

According to a survey conducted in 1955, forty-two per cent of the new homes in America do not have bookshelves. Only seventeen per cent of American adults over twenty-one years of age read one book a year. Twenty-five per cent of college graduates do not read one book a year in addition to their professional requirements. Does serious reading have a place in your daily schedule? Do you read the Bible?

One of the most stirring scenes of Holy Writ is found in the fourth chapter of Luke. Jesus was in Nazareth and, according to his custom, went to the synagogue to worship. As a visiting religious teacher he was invited to read from the sacred Scriptures. When he finished ". . . he closed the book, and gave it back to the attendant, and sat down; and the eyes of all in the synagogue were fixed on him. And he began to say to them, 'Today this scripture has been fulfilled in your hearing.'" (Luke 4:20-21.)

We can be sure that Jesus had opened the Book many times prior to this occasion. Indeed, he had absorbed it. With the coming of Jesus the old Book was now closed in consummation. It had revealed as much of God as it was possible to reveal. When Jesus closed the Book, the people saw him. He was the fulfillment of the Book and of God's saving purposes for men.

The New York Times carried an advertisement designed to encourage the buying of Israeli bonds. The full-page spread carried a large picture of a Jewish Torah bearing on its cover the words, "Behind Israel is a Book." Indeed! Behind Christianity is a Book and we ought to be familiar with it. But let us not forget that behind Christianity—yea, beyond it—is a Life, the Man of the centuries, the Man, Christ Jesus.

As professing Christians, what a pity it would be to come to the close of the year without looking back at the church.

Sometimes it is most difficult to catalogue its accomplishments. Then again perhaps in times of great stress, we see this great institution in all of its glory. Standing in the waning hours of the year and looking back, what do you see?

In his brilliant and penetrating book, *And There Was Light*, Rudolf Thiel devotes a chapter to "The New Universe." In it he discusses space travel. He reminds us that Kepler's fable of a voyage to the Moon is receiving more and more serious attention from earnest mathematicians and scientists. Dr. Thiel maintains that the most serious problem involved in anticipated space travel is that of overcoming the Earth's gravitation. This, he asserts, will necessitate the development of speed ten times greater than the "top velocities yet obtained by airplanes." Assuming that proper conditions were met for a trip to the Moon, the eminent German astronomer says it would require five days. Then he claims it would take about two hundred sixty days to reach Mars. There, explorers would have to wait some fifteen months for the Earth's closest approach for a return trip. The duration of "the entire voyage would be two and one-half years." Dr. Thiel makes this arresting comment: "Apparently, the outlook is unexpectedly good. We need only the vantage point outside the Earth that Archimedes called for—not to move the world, but to escape from it."[2]

Let us, therefore, continue the speculation by reversing the voyage and let us imagine that *we* had a visitor from outer space. Momentarily such a guest would lose perspective while scanning the powerful and fascinating American skyline. Certainly he would go to our historic shrines and chambers of law. Wall Street would, no doubt, startle him if New York

---

[2]From *And There Was Light*, by Rudolf Thiel. Copyright 1957 by Alfred A. Knopf, Inc. Used by permission.

traffic did not. To be sure, a citizen from beyond the horizon would be impressed with America's courage, technical skill, resources, and confidence.

But what would the guest from outer space think of the church? To him there would doubtless be a shocking contrast between the skill and devotion of the secular world and the spirit and devotion manifested on the part of the church. Let it be said that no visitor from outer space, nor inhabitant of this planet, can objectively analyze the church. It defies graphs and charts. As Truman B. Douglass says, "The Church cannot be seen at all if it is seen only objectively. To see it, one has to get inside. One has to be involved—to *care* about the Church and what it stands for."[3]

As you look back over the year, to what extent did you become involved in the witness of the church? The Oberlin Conference and the Fourth Assembly of the National Council of Churches in St. Louis should remind us of the inconceivable dimensions of the church. Ecumenical Christianity speaks of the essential oneness of the church.

To those who are involved in the church there are definite areas of observable progress. Statisticians declare that for the first time there are more than 100,000,000 members of the church in the United States. A century ago only two persons in ten belonged to the church. Today, about six in ten are identified with the Christian community. It is claimed that 52.5 per cent of professing Christians go to church at least occasionally. Protestant and Eastern Orthodox Churches raised and handled $2,043,741,555 in the calendar year 1956.[4] Though this is a tremendous sum of money, the fact remains that less

---

[3]From *Why Go to Church?* by Truman B. Douglass. Copyright 1957, by Harper & Brothers.

[4]See *Statistics of Giving,* Department of Stewardship and Benevolence, National Council of Churches of Christ in the U.S.A., New York, November, 1957.

than two per cent of America's income reaches America's churches.

Review the local scene. How involved did you permit yourself to become in *your* church during the year? Did you "play it safe," or were you willing to gamble for God?

King Henry IV once called Crillon "the bravest of the brave." Later, however, he sent this dogmatic word to the old soldier: "Hang yourself, brave Crillon: We have fought at Arques and you were not there."

As the year ends, Christians must also face the scrutiny of this criticism. As always the church has been on the firing line for justice, decency, good will, and brotherhood. Were you there?

In the struggle to recruit and train leadership for the church, were you there?

In the suicidal armament race, did you lift your voice in protest or write a single letter to your senator?

In the battle for Civil Rights, did you try to remain a dignified neutral or did you take a Christian stand for the human race?

In the struggle for peace and good will, did you through your business and personal practice contribute to conditions that breed war or promote peace?

In the areas of law enforcement and good citizenship, did you join in the struggle for impartial justice, or did you thank God that the legislation did not apply to you?

In the realm of material things, did you rob God to get ahead? Did you deny the church its due?

In retrospect, was the church the means of expressing your faith in Jesus Christ, or did it complicate your schedule and injure your pride?

As C. Kilmer Myers has said, "People must come to understand that a parish not in tension is not, in our day, a Christian parish. One reason that makes this so, is that churches have lost their ultimate vision. . ."[5] In this context, is *your* church in tension? Even more personal, do you want *your* church in tension for Jesus Christ?

---

[5]From *Light the Dark Streets,* by C. Kilmer Myers. Copyright, 1957, by the Seabury Press. Used by permission.

What Is God Like?

"The God who made the world and everything in it, being Lord of heaven and earth, does not live in shrines made by man, nor is he served by human hands, as though he needed anything, since he himself gives to all men life and breath and everything."

—Acts 17:24-25

T H E   F A M I L Y had gone to the mountains for vacation. Their cottage overlooked a friendly lake. After a swim and dinner, it was bedtime. Tenderly, the mother prepared her little daughter for the night: heard her prayers, kissed her, and left the room. Immediately, Julia called for her to come back. The child raised some difficult questions about God. Patiently, the mother listened and then said reassuringly, "We'll be on the porch. There's nothing to hurt you. God is in the dark as well as in the light." Plaintively, the child replied, "But I can't see him in the dark, Mummy. I want a God with a face."

So do we all. When night comes, trouble knocks, disappointments punctuate the day, and problems pyramid, we all crave a God with a face. In our anxiety and agony, we join David in saying,

Such is the generation of those who seek him,
who seek the face of the God of Jacob.

—Psalm 24:6

What, then, is God like? J. B. Phillips has suggested that to many people he is a policeman, constantly patrolling the beat of life. He is out to watch us, if not to catch us, in an unguarded moment. But certainly God represents more than law.

Is God like conscience? Can we really equate conscience with God? Our sensitivity to right and wrong is usually synonymous with personal experience. To be sure, God speaks to us through conscience, but let us not forget: We do not always listen, nor do we answer.

To some, God is a grand old man, comfortably situated in heaven. He was a source of real assistance and joy to our forefathers. But there is some question if he will be able to keep pace with our supersonic age. God is growing old.

God is imagined to be a persistent professor, who takes great pleasure in giving final examinations to his unprepared students. If there is a way to fail them, he will.

There are those who look upon God much as they would on insurance, an investment in the future. God is not insurance; he is assurance.

None of these creations of the mind is adequate to give solace and strength in time of need. For, as the writer of Acts has so clearly stated, " 'We ought not to think that the Deity is like gold, or silver, or stone, a representation by the art and imagination of man.' " (Acts 17:29.)

Whereas, "No one has ever seen God. . ." (John 1:18) there are definite portrayals and pictures that incite the imagination and reassure us of his nature and presence.

Speaking more positively, to know God is to accept him as indescribable and indestructible beauty. He is the creator and operator of the world. This is not pantheism, but rather the ability to recognize and accept the marvels of nature as the royal garments of God.

God is like the flowering meadow; birds on wing; quail calling at nightfall. He is like a babbling brook, down whose pebbled bottom walk barefoot children.

God is like a virgin forest, immense, straight and strong and silent; like a beautifully tilled field or a granary running over. He is like a majestic mountain in the distance, that appears to be upholding the sky; like a turbulent sea, seeking its level; like an angry night sky with forked lightning streaking its face.

He is like the freshness of wind-driven snow, clinging to an unpainted barn. He is as friendly as sunshine after a freeze; as delightful as dawn after a fitful night. God is like an inexhaustible geyser, filling the world with refreshing atmosphere. He is like a cool spring along a dusty road; like a shade tree in the desert. He is like a tear in mercy shed; like laughter amid exuberant joy.

Whether in the designs and rhythms of nature or in demonstrations of personal compassion, beauty in any and every form is like God.

William L. Stidger has glimpsed the grandeur of God in these descriptive lines:

> I saw God wash the world last night
>   With his sweet showers on high,
> And then, when morning came, I saw
>   Him hang it out to dry.
>
> He washed each tiny blade of grass,
>   And every trembling tree;
> He flung his showers against the hill,
>   And swept the billowing sea.

The white rose is a cleaner white,
    The red rose is more red,
Since God washed every fragrant face
    And put them all to bed.

There's not a bird; there's not a bee
    That wings along the way
But is a cleaner bird and bee
    Than it was yesterday.

I saw God wash the world last night.
    Ah, would He had washed me
As clean of all my dust and dirt
    As that old white birch tree.[1]

God is power. His invisible, yet available, power moves the world. Theologians refer to God as omnipotent—having unlimited power. Ours is a day of power. Both the atom and the automobile hold our attention. With the splitting of the atom has come the multiplication of unimagined power and speed. That which pleases a prospective buyer of an automobile is not only its make and design, but its horsepower.

In such a technical age it would seem that we could comprehend God more clearly when he is expressed in terms of power. But the deduction is not that simple, for the only power that many know is engineered power, external power, measurable power.

We stood one day atop Jewel Ridge in southwest Virginia. Although we were between two powerful generators, we could hear each other talk. Over the ridge, a few miles away, the current from this plant was illuminating and furnishing the energy for a coal mine. The motors were throbbing. The indicators pointed to the voltage. From a very delicate instrument flowed a ribbon of paper in the form of a graph, show-

---

[1]Copyright 1934 by The Rodeheaver Co.

ing the operator the amount of electricity being consumed. We stood in the presence of the miracle of electricity.

God is like that silent, transforming power. His truth illuminates the world. History is his graph and men his way. Furthermore, God has promised to energize man, to imbue him with spiritual power even more miraculous than electricity. If we have learned anything from this atomic age, it is the vulnerability of the visible and the stability of the invisible.

Faith is power. Here is the assurance: "But to all who received him, who believed in his name, he gave power to become children of God. . ." (John 1:12.)

God is limitless love. The writer of 1 John says, "He who does not love does not know God, for God is love." (4:8.) Love is most difficult to define. Its manifestations and demonstrations are more easily discernible.

The saintly Toyohiko Kagawa speaks of the laws of love and begins with instinctive love. This is demonstrated by a mother's love for her children; a man's love for his wife. Then there is moral love: a love for righteousness and goodness which impels one to identify himself with the highest and the best which he is capable of comprehending. It also demands of him to be kind and considerate and compassionate. The highest level of love, to continue with Kagawa's thinking, is "supermoral" love: We must love the corrupt sinner. We must love people regardless of their class, color, or condition.

But you ask, "If God is love, how can you justify poisonous snakes and insects, treacherous mountains, perilous seas, disease-infested swamps, and burning deserts? How can you picture God as love when suffering and injustice and misery continue? How can God be understanding love when men continue to persecute one another and nations kill off their young?" Love is always a paradox. Frequently we, too, cry out,

"My soul also is sorely troubled.
But thou, O LORD—how long?" (Psalm 6:3.)

Then Whittier's affirmation in "The Eternal Goodness" is reassuring:

I see the wrong that round me lies,
   I feel the guilt within;
I hear, with groan and travail-cries,
   The world confess its sin.

Yet, in the maddening maze of things,
   And tossed by storm and flood,
To one fixed trust my spirit clings;
   I know that God is good!

.   .   .   .

And so beside the Silent Sea,
   I wait the muffled oar;
No harm from Him can come to me
   On ocean or on shore.

I know not where His islands lift
   Their fronded palms in air;
I only know I cannot drift
   Beyond His love and care.

Weatherhead tells the story of a British soldier who asked his officer's permission to retrieve his wounded buddy from "No Man's Land." He retorted, "No, of course you can't. Look at the firing. . . Nobody could live out there. Your friend is mortally wounded; if you go, you'll be mortally wounded too, and I'll lose both of you."

But later, the young man dashed out into the night. He crawled, jumped, and ran across the area until he found his friend. With great difficulty he placed him on his shoulder and, though wounded, staggered back toward the British trenches. His officer met him with this sharp reprimand: "I told you! I told you it wasn't worth it. He's dead, and you're mortally wounded, just as I said."

The panting, bleeding soldier turned his dying eyes toward the officer's face and replied, "It was worth it, sir."

"Worth it?" shouted the officer.

"It was worth it because when I got to him he said, 'Jim, I knew you'd come.' "[2]

Love is like that. God is like that. He always comes to us, whatever the need.

God is our common Father. It is possible to ascribe to God personal attributes without defining him as a giant. With the advancement of the race and specifically with the reign of the prophets of Israel—like Amos, Hosea, Jeremiah, and Isaiah —came fresh and meaningful characteristics of Jehovah. By his actions God was known as justice, love, suffering, mercy, and holiness. The finest and the best in man were associated with God, because personal existence was and still is the loftiest type of existence.

Jesus thought of God most commonly as Father. This does not mean that he is a magnified image of anyone's father— some fathers would scarcely qualify. I am reminded of the little boy who said, "God is like my father; he is too busy to listen." But the relationship that exists between God and his children is more easily understood in terms of wonderful family relationships.

---

[2] From "Turning the Corner," in *Great Preaching Today.* Copyright 1955 by Harper & Brothers. Used by permission.

Have you ever thought through these searching words of Christ: "Or what man of you, if his son asks him for a loaf, will give him a stone? Or if he asks for a fish, will give him a serpent? If you then, who are evil, know how to give good gifts to your children, how much more will your Father who is in heaven give good things to those who ask him." (Matthew 7:9-11.)

Furthermore, Jesus told his disciples to address their prayers to the common Father. His great prayer begins with the words, "Our Father. . . ."

One of the most beautiful parables ever told is that of the prodigal son. In reality, it is a picture of God the Father and man—the most winsome ever painted. He is here pictured as a concerned, loving, forgiving Father, utterly willing to restore and to redeem.

A modern parable is an incident which occurred between the late Burris A. Jenkins, noted Disciple author and preacher, and his father. While Burris was in college, his father admonished him not to join a certain fraternity. The son secretly became a member. For four years he lived with that secret. Then one evening, as he was speaking to a group of young people, he suddenly realized his unworthiness. The following day, Burris Jenkins wrote his father and told him everything. Whereupon he received this telegram: "It's all right. I forgive you. I knew it two days after you did it. Love, Father."

God is like that.

God is like Jesus who is our clearest revelation of the Father. "God was in Christ reconciling the world to himself. . ." (2 Corinthians 5:19.) In the Fourth Gospel, our Lord declared, " 'I and the Father are one.' " (John 10:30.) And again in the same Gospel, anxious Philip asked, " 'Lord, show us the Father, and we shall be satisfied.' Jesus said to him, 'Have I been with you so long, and yet you do not know me, Philip?

He who has seen me has seen the Father; how can you say, "Show us the Father"?' " (John 14:9.)

Christ came to reveal God. Indeed, he was God focused in the flesh. The Great Physician came to introduce man to "wholeness of life." He taught as never a man taught. He healed as man had never before healed. He forgave when retaliation would have been easier. He outlived any other man. He outdied his enemies. As Renan has said, "Whatever the surprises of history, Jesus will never be surpassed."

He died voluntarily. Luther once suggested that every seeker should begin thinking "at the wounds of Christ." And this is, paradoxically enough, the conclusion and the beginning of the entire matter. For as Paul expressed it, "He died for all, that those who live might live no longer for themselves but for him who for their sake died and was raised." (2 Corinthians 5:25.)

Charles B. Templeton tells of an experience of King Edward VII of England. He and his queen were out walking late one afternoon when suddenly she stumbled and sprained her ankle. In great pain and with considerable difficulty, she limped along, holding to her husband's shoulder.

At dusk, they approached the home of a humble man. The king knocked on the door. "Who's there?" came the query.

"It is Edward. It is the king. Let me in."

The man on the inside shouted back, "Enough of your pranks now. Be off. . . ."

The king, not being accustomed to such language, was astounded. He hardly knew what to do, but he knocked a second time. The cottager inquired, "What do you want?"

"I tell you it is the king! It is Edward, your king. Let me in."

In anger the man retorted, "I'll teach you to torment an honest man trying to get his sleep." He threw open the door in disgust, only to see that indeed it was his king! With profuse apologies the laborer invited the royal visitors in and sent for help to attend his queen.

Years later, when the Britisher was too old to work, he would spend much time rocking on the porch and visiting with his neighbors. He took great delight in reviewing that experience, always concluding with the same words: "And to think, to think, I almost didn't let him in! To think I almost didn't let him in!"[3]

" ' "Behold, I stand at the door and knock; if any one hears my voice and opens the door, I will come in to him and eat with him, and he with me." ' " (Revelation 3:20.)

Not until you open your heart and let Jesus in, will you know what God is like.

---

[3]From "God Believes in You," by Charles B. Templeton. Copyrighted by the Christian Century Foundation and reprinted by permission of *The Pulpit*, from the issue of February, 1953.

Starting Blocks

I N   T R A C K, starting blocks are adjustable steel contrivances against which the runner plants his feet while crouching in position for the race, thus being assured of a firm and fast start with the crack of the gun. The blocks, however, do not determine the speed of the runner; their only value is to give a satisfactory start.

The following topics and texts of possible sermons for special seasons and occasions are offered with the hope that they may assist the busy minister.

THE NEW YEAR

Beginning with God

In the beginning God created the heavens and the earth.

—Genesis 1:1

Doors of Destiny

" 'I know your works. Behold, I have set before you an open door, which no one is able to shut; I know that you have but little power, and yet you have kept my word and have not denied my name.' "

—Revelation 3:8

Facing the Future with Faith

Brethren, I do not consider that I have made it my own; but one thing I do, forgetting what lies behind and straining forward to what lies ahead, I press on toward the goal for the prize of the upward call of God in Christ Jesus.

—Philippians 3:13-14

UNIVERSAL WEEK OF PRAYER

On Praying to Yourself

"The Pharisee stood and prayed thus with himself, 'God, I thank thee that I am not like other men.' "

—Luke 18:11

The Ministry of Prayer

You also must help us by prayer, so that many will give thanks on our behalf for the blessing granted us in answer to many prayers.

—2 Corinthians 1:11

How Long Do You Pray?

In these days he went out into the hills to pray; and all night he continued in prayer to God.

—Luke 6:12

YOUTH WEEK

On Growing Up

And the child grew and became strong, filled with wisdom; and the favor of God was upon him.

—Luke 2:40

Remember Who You Are

"You are the light of the world. A city set on a hill cannot be hid."

—Matthew 5:14

What's in It for Me?

Then Peter said in reply, "Lo, we have left everything and followed you. What then shall we have?"

—Matthew 19:27

BROTHERHOOD WEEK

For the Healing of the Nations

. . . and the leaves of the tree were for the healing of the nations.

—Revelation 22:2

A Time for Compassion

As he landed he saw a great throng, and he had compassion on them, because they were like sheep without a shepherd; and he began to teach them many things.

—Mark 6:34

Your Brother's Keeper

Then the LORD said to Cain, "Where is Abel your brother?" He said, "I do not know; am I my brother's keeper?"

—Genesis 4:9

FOREIGN MISSIONS DAY

The World Mission of the Church

"Go therefore and make disciples of all nations, baptizing them in the name of the Father and of the Son and of the Holy Spirit, teaching them to observe all that I have commanded you; and lo, I am with you always, to the close of the age."

—Matthew 28:19-20

One Gospel for One World

"And this gospel of the kingdom will be preached throughout the whole world, . . ."

—Matthew 24:14

Witnesses

". . . you shall be my witnesses in Jerusalem and in all Judea and Samaria and to the end of the earth."

—Acts 1:8

HOLY WEEK

On Entering Our Jerusalems

When the days drew near for him to be received up, he set his face to go to Jerusalem. And he sent messengers ahead of him.

—Luke 9:51

Himself He Could Not Save

So also the chief priests mocked him to one another with the scribes, saying, "He saved others; he cannot save himself."

—Mark 15:31

The Cross of Christ in a Chrome-plated Society

For Jews demand signs and Greeks seek wisdom, but we preach Christ crucified, a stumbling-block to Jews and folly to Gentiles.

—1 Corinthians 1:22-23

EASTER

The Voice that Wakes the Dead

"Truly, truly, I say to you, the hour is coming, and now is, when the dead will hear the voice of the Son of God, and those who hear will live."

—John 5:25

Good Morning!

And Jesus himself met them, and said, "Good morning!"

—Matthew 28:9 (Goodspeed)

You Can't Afford to Die

". . . and whoever lives and believes in me shall never die. Do you believe this?"

—John 11:26

CHRISTIAN HIGHER EDUCATION DAY

The Church and Christian Education

"I am a Jew, born at Tarsus in Cilicia, but brought up in this city at the feet of Gamaliel, educated according to the strict manner of the law of our fathers, being zealous for God as you all are this day."

—Acts 22:3

What the Church Expects of the College

. . . youths without blemish, handsome and skilful in all wisdom, endowed with knowledge, understanding learning, and competent to serve in the king's palace, and to teach them the letters and language of the Chaldeans.

—Daniel 1:4

What the College Expects of the Church

I will send those whom you accredit by letter to carry your gift to Jerusalem.

—1 Corinthians 16:3

RURAL LIFE SUNDAY

God's Good Earth

The earth is the Lord's and the
fulness thereof,
the world and those who dwell
therein.

—Psalm 24:1

A Farmer's Faith

"A sower went out to sow."

—Mark 4:3

Big Men and Little Towns

"Can anything good come out of Nazareth?"

—John 1:46

CHRISTIAN FAMILY WEEK

The Crown of Motherhood

Go forth, O daughters of Zion,
and behold King Solomon,
with the crown with which his mother crowned him
on the day of his wedding,
on the day of the gladness of his heart.

—Song of Solomon 3:11

Love Never Bargains

Love is patient and kind; love is not jealous or boastful; it is not arrogant or rude.   Love does not insist on its own way; it is not irritable or resentful.

—1 Corinthians 13:4-5

Magnificent Marriages

Let marriage be held in honor.

—Hebrews 13:4

PENTECOST

The Power of Togetherness

When the day of Pentecost had come, they were all together in one place.

—Acts 2:1

When Pentecost Becomes Personal

It was at that time that Peter got up among the brothers—there were about a hundred and twenty persons present—and said, . . .

—Acts 1:15 (Goodspeed)

MEMORIAL DAY

God Save America

Blessed is the nation whose God is the LORD.

—Psalm 33:12a

Peace and Power

"Peace I leave with you; my peace I give to you; not as the world gives do I give to you. Let not your hearts be troubled, neither let them be afraid."

—John 14:27

They Flung the Torch to Us

For Zion's sake I will keep silent.
    and for Jerusalem's sake I will not rest,
until her vindication goes forth as brightness,
    and her salvation as a burning torch.

—Isaiah 62:1

Therefore let us be grateful for receiving a kingdom that cannot be shaken, and thus let us offer to God acceptable worship, with reverence and awe; for our God is a consuming fire.

—Hebrews 12:28-29

BUDGET SUNDAY

Unpurchaseable Men

But King David said to Ornan, "No, but I will buy it for the full price; I will not take for the LORD what is yours, nor offer burnt offerings which cost me nothing."

—1 Chronicles 21:24

Manager or Messenger?

"The land of a rich man brought forth plentifully; . . ."

—Luke 12:16a

Tipping or Tithing?

"Will man rob God? Yet you are robbing me. But you say, 'How are we robbing thee?' In your tithes and offerings."

—Malachi 3:8

CHILDREN'S DAY

There Is a Lad Here

"There is a lad here who has five barley loaves and two fish; but what are they among so many?"

—John 6:9

The Church in Your Home

"Return to your home, and declare how much God has done for you." And he went away, proclaiming throughout the whole city how much Jesus had done for him.

—Luke 8:39

Christian Maturity

"To what then shall I compare the men of this generation, and what are they like? They are like children sitting in the market place and calling to one another,

'We piped to you, and you did not dance;
we wailed, and you did not weep.'"

—Luke 7:31-32

GRADUATION WEEK

Needed: New Men

Therefore, if any one is in Christ, he is a new creation; the old has passed away, behold, the new has come.

—2 Corinthians 5:17

On Leaving the Ivory Towers

Your neck is like an ivory tower.
Your eyes are pools in Heshbon,
by the gate of Bath-rabbim.
Your nose is like a tower of Lebanon,
overlooking Damascus.

—Song of Solomon 7:4

Are You in Orbit?

I mean, brethren, the appointed time has grown very short.

—1 Corinthians 7:29a

FATHER'S DAY

Father and Son

"Do not lay your hand on the lad or do anything to him; for now I know that you fear God."

—Genesis 22:12

A Father's Failure

"O my son Absalom, my son, my son, Absalom! Would I had died instead of you, O Absalom, my son, my son!"

—2 Samuel 18:33b

Mighty Men

These were the mighty men that were of old, the men of renown.

—Genesis 6:4

ACHIEVEMENT OR ANNIVERSARY SUNDAY

Magnificent Memories

Remember Jesus Christ, risen from the dead, descended from David, as preached in my gospel.

—2 Timothy 2:8

The Church Beneath the Cross

It is those who want to make a good showing in the flesh that would compel you to be circumcised, and only in order that they may not be persecuted for the cross of Christ.

—Galatians 6:12

How Large Is Your Church?

Then I was given a measuring rod like a staff, and I was told: "Rise and measure the temple of God and the altar and those who worship there."

—Revelation 11:1

INSTALLATION SUNDAY

The Official Board

These they set before the apostles, and they prayed and laid their hands upon them.

—Acts 6:6

"Called in Honor"

. . . love one another with brotherly affection; outdo one another in showing honor.

—Romans 12:10

The Testimony of Teaching

For I would have you know, brethren, that the gospel which was preached by me is not man's gospel. For I did not receive it from man, nor was I taught it, but it came through a revelation of Jesus Christ.

—Galatians 1:11-12

FREEDOM AND DEMOCRACY SUNDAY

"Our Common Glory"

"The glory which thou hast given me I have given to them, that they may be one even as we are one."

—John 17:22

The Conceit of Communism
They promise them freedom, but they themselves are slaves of corruption; for whatever overcomes a man, to that he is enslaved.

—2 Peter 2:19

Toward an Understanding of Freedom
"and you will know the truth, and the truth will make you free."

—John 8:32

LABOR SUNDAY
What's Your Line?
Do your best to present yourself to God as one approved, a workman who has no need to be ashamed, rightly handling the word of truth.

—2 Timothy 2:15

Do You Work in Gloves?
The Lord said to him, "What is that in your hand?"

—Exodus 4:2

God's Labor Union
Greet those workers in the Lord.

—Romans 16:12

GO-TO-COLLEGE SUNDAY
Some Keys to Learning
"Woe to you lawyers! for you have taken away the key of knowledge; you did not enter yourselves, and you hindered those who were entering."

—Luke 11:52

When Is a Man Educated?
Have this mind among yourselves, which you have in Christ Jesus.

—Philippians 2:5

The Campus and the Church
And Manoah said, "Now when your words come true, what is to be the boy's manner of life, and what is he to do?"

—Judges 13:12

WORLD-WIDE COMMUNION SUNDAY
Symbols that Speak
And he said to the people of Israel, "When your children ask their fathers in time to come, 'What do these stones mean?' then you shall let your children know, 'Israel passed over this Jordan on dry ground."

—Joshua 4:21-22

"Bread for the World in Mercy Broken"
They said to him, "Lord, give us this bread always."

—John 6:34

Cup of the New Covenant

And he took a cup, and when he had given thanks he gave it to them, and they all drank of it.

—Mark 14:23

THE WEEK OF THE MINISTRY
The Uniqueness of the Ministry

"The Spirit of the Lord is upon me, because he has anointed me to preach. . ."

—Luke 4:18

Our Common Ministry

"See that you fulfill the ministry which you have received in the Lord."

—Colossians 4:17

The Ministry of Jesus

But as it is, Christ has obtained a ministry which is as much more excellent than the old as the covenant he mediates is better, since it is enacted on better promises.

—Hebrews 8:6

LAYMEN'S SUNDAY
Committed Churchmen

They stood every man in his place round about the camp, and all the army ran; they cried out and fled.

—Judges 7:21

Christianity: a Layman's Religion

Now those who were scattered went about preaching the word.

—Acts 8:4

How Strong Are the Strong?

". . . our God whom we serve is able. . ."

—Daniel 3:17

REFORMATION SUNDAY
To What Church Do You Belong?

So he argued in the synagogue with the Jews and the devout persons, and in the market place every day with those who chanced to be there.

—Acts 17:17

Pillars of Protestantism

. . . you may know how one ought to behave in the household of God, which is the church of the living God, the pillar and bulwark of the truth. Great indeed, we confess, is the mystery of our religion.

—1 Timothy 3:15-16a

The Coming Great Church

. . . that the church might be presented before him in splendor, without spot or wrinkle or any such thing, that she might be holy and without blemish.

—Ephesians 5:27

ELECTION WEEK

My Favorite Candidate

". . . I have found no fault in him to this day."

—1 Samuel 29:3

"I find no crime in him."

—John 18:38b

The Church and Politics

Live like free men, only do not make your freedom a pretext for misconduct; live like servants of God.

—1 Peter 2:16 (Moffatt)

Responsible Citizenship

So the tribune came and said to him, "Tell me, are you a Roman citizen?" And he said, "Yes." The tribune answered, "I bought this citizenship for a large sum." Paul said, "But I was born a citizen."

—Acts 22:27-28

THANKSGIVING

On Being Grateful

Then one of them, when he saw that he was healed, turned back, praising God with a loud voice; and he fell on his face at Jesus' feet, giving him thanks.

—Luke 17:15-16

Faith of Our Fathers

Therefore, since we are surrounded by so great a cloud of witnesses, let us also lay aside every weight, and sin which clings so closely, and let us run with perseverance the race that is set before us, looking to Jesus the pioneer and perfecter of our faith, who for the joy that was set before him endured the cross, despising the shame, and is seated at the right hand of the throne of God.

—Hebrews 12:1-2

"Remembrance Rock"

Blessed is the nation whose God is the LORD,
the people whom he has chosen as his heritage!

—Psalm 33:12

WOMAN'S DAY

Wonderful Women

For it is all for your sake, so that as grace extends to more and more people it may increase thanksgiving, to the glory of God.

—2 Corinthians 4:15

Committed to Us

But thanks be to God, that you who were once slaves of sin have become obedient from the heart to the standard of teaching to which you were committed, and, having been set free from sin, have become slaves of righteousness.

—Romans 6:17-18

UNIVERSAL BIBLE SUNDAY

The Living Word

And the Word became flesh and dwelt among us, full of grace and truth; we have beheld his glory, glory as of the only Son from the Father.

—John 1:14

What Do You Read?

And when they read it, they rejoiced at the exhortation.

—Acts 15:31

Toward an Understanding of the Bible

"Do you understand what you are reading?"

—Acts 8:30

CHRISTMAS

Concerning This Child

And when they saw it they made known the saying which had been told them concerning this child.

—Luke 2:17

Are You Ready for Christmas?

And she gave birth to her first-born son and wrapped him in swaddling cloths, and laid him in a manger, because there was no place for them in the inn.

—Luke 2:7

"Be Born in Us Today"

O holy Child of Bethlehem! Descend to us, we pray;
Cast out our sin, and enter in,
Be born in us today.

—Phillips Brooks

LAST SUNDAY IN THE YEAR

On Looking Back

But Lot's wife behind him looked back, and she became a pillar of salt.

—Genesis 19:26

Between the Years

And they stood still, looking sad.

—Luke 24:17

On Changing Your Mind

Do not be conformed to this world but be transformed by the renewal of your mind, that you may prove what is the will of God, what is good and acceptable and perfect.

—Romans 12:2

LAST SUNDAY IN OLD PULPIT

The Church I Should Like to Leave My Successor

. . . that the church might be presented before him in splendor, without spot or wrinkle or any such thing, that she might be holy and without blemish.

—Ephesians 6:27

"Time to Remember"

I thank my God in all my remembrance of you, always in every prayer of mine for you all making my prayer with joy, thankful for your partnership in the gospel from the first day until now.

—Philippians 1:3-5

Foundations for the Future

. . . thus laying up for themselves good foundations for the future, so that they may take hold of the life which is life indeed.

—1 Timothy 6:19

FIRST SUNDAY IN A NEW PULPIT

Assumptions and Assurances

. . . assuming that you have heard of the stewardship of God's grace that was given to me for you.

—Ephesians 3:2

On Knowing Jesus

For I decided to know nothing among you except Jesus Christ and him crucified.

—1 Corinthians 2:2

"I Believe"

"I believe; help my unbelief!"

—Mark 9:24

G. Curtis Jones

Dr. Jones has been pastor of Union Avenue Christian Church in St. Louis since 1955. He is the author of seven other popular books.

Before coming to St. Louis he served churches in Tennessee, Virginia, Michigan, and North Carolina.

Dr. Jones received his BA degree from Lynchburg College and BD degree from Yale University Divinity School. In 1948 he was awarded an honorary DD degree from Lynchburg College.

In addition to being a world traveler, he is a popular preacher and lecturer before ministers, college groups, and annual interdenominational meetings.

He is a member of the Board of Directors of the Metropolitan Church Federation of Greater St. Louis, the Division of Christian Education of the National Council of Churches, Unified Promotion Inc., and The Disciples of Christ Historical Society.

Other books by Dr. Jones are *Repairing Our Religion, On Being Your Best, In Their Light We Walk, Which Way Is Progress? What Are You Worth? What Are You Doing?* and *Youth Deserves to Know.*